MARRIED TO ITALY:
LOVE, LIES AND LEGAL NIGHTMARES

WRITTEN BY

LUCINDA FAULKNER

Copyright © *Lucinda Faulkner,* 2025
All Rights Reserved

This book is subject to the condition that no part of this book is to be reproduced, transmitted in any form or means; electronic or mechanical, stored in a retrieval system, photocopied, recorded, scanned, or otherwise. Any of these actions require the proper written permission of the author.

TABLE OF CONTENTS

Chapter 1 1
Chapter 2 3
Chapter 3 7
Chapter 4 9
Chapter 5 14
Chapter 6 16
Chapter 7 20
Chapter 8 24
Chapter 9 27
Chapter 10 30
Chapter 11 33
Chapter 12 35
Chapter 13 38
Chapter 14 51
Chapter 15 56
Chapter 16 58
Chapter 17 61
Chapter 18 66
Chapter 19 69
Chapter 20 72
Chapter 21 75
Chapter 22 82
Chapter 23 89
Chapter 24 93
Chapter 25 102
Chapter 26 108
Chapter 27 111

Chapter 28 115
Chapter 29 119
Chapter 30 122
Chapter 31 127
Chapter 32 132
Chapter 33 137
Chapter 34 139

Italy: The land of romance, rolling vineyards, and bureaucratic nightmares so intricate that Dante would have written an extra level of hell just for them.

Italy: The land where men are poetic until they get what they want, then suddenly forget how to text back.

The one where the legal system is so slow that by the time you get to a court date, you've aged out of the outfit you bought for it. The one where everything should work but somehow….doesn't.

Italy: Getting married and then trying to untangle yourself from a country that loves drama more than it loves efficiency.

A tale of romance, betrayal, and the absurdity of trying to get justice in a place where even getting a plumber requires divine intervention.

Italy: The highs of a honeymoon phase full of charming accents, endless plates of pasta, and the lows of a divorce process so long and painful it could qualify as an Olympic sport.

Lawyers who never showed up, judges who took decade-long lunch breaks, and the Italian men who - spoiler alert - turned out to be more interested in themselves than in love.

So, if you've ever fantasised about running off to Italy for a whirlwind romance, let this book be your warning label. And if you're already here, trapped in a legal battle that makes Kafka look like light reading - welcome to the club.

Grab a glass of wine. You're going to need it.

CHAPTER 1

Having moved to Italy many years ago, at a time when a computer didn't exist nor did Sky TV, my decision was rather a risk, and any information about the country was to be found in library books or magazines.

Now, with the internet and well-made documentaries on TV, we can all see how the other half live.

Just lately, a few British-made programs on life in Italy have been on Sky channels, and although I have been living here a lifetime and know by now how things work, I was very curious to see how Italy was portrayed from a UK point of view. Plus, watching something in my own language is always a pleasure.

Although the programs were broadcast in the UK months before they got to us, it is still interesting to see the picture they portray. The UK commentator takes us to places we dream of going to someday, and everything seems like paradise.

The programs are very well made, but each episode is very much based on luxury and of course, showing us around all the best places in the best possible situations.

The British guide travels around in five-star luxury situations and is treated like a VIP wherever he goes, which is not very real, in my opinion.

Anyone who has managed to save up or has money can have a lovely five-star holiday and see the best. They can be treated like a king or a queen and be wrapped in paradise as a tourist for a while. But what about real life? Is it really like this as they portray in their documentaries?

Of course, they have to do their best to get people interested for the sake of tourism, but a little bit of real life too would not go amiss if you really want to find out about a country, don't you think?

Anyhow, after seeing a few of these documentaries, I decided to do something of my own. Not to put people off coming to the country, which, of course, has its beauty and good points, but to give an insight as to what real life is like over here, and it certainly is not a dream as so many people would have us believe! The traditions, the mentality, their likes and dislikes, how families work, and above all, the dreaded, wicked mothers-in-law! So many real things that just cannot be seen in documentaries.

CHAPTER 2

Growing up in the wonderful countryside in the East of England couldn't have been better, so why do we always think that the grass is greener on the other side?

Is there any comparison between living in the countryside and living in a dirty, grey, smoggy town, cooped up in what resembles a rabbit hutch with people living on top of you, underneath and side by side, where you can literally hear everything going on? You can hear their telephone calls and even when they go to the bathroom!

Why ever did I leave, I ask myself, remembering the lovely summer evenings and walks in the countryside, the silence and the fresh, clean breeze. My friends were my animals and my garden was like a zoo with ducks, geese, dogs and cats and of course my horse. A very normal country life, which I soon came to realise once in Italy, was actually a luxury which I had never considered as so.

My personal life had taken a bad turn, and with what information one could acquire watching idyllic documentaries on TV and my wish to learn a language, I made my decision. There were no computers and internet for me when I was young, so television or books were the only source of learning.

I had let my desire to study a language impair my judgement, and it was the worst decision that I could have made.

At that time, not particularly brilliant at school. I never really knew how much I loved languages or that I could even accomplish learning one and so the usual routine of growing up, going to college, leaving home at 18 and then living with someone just went ahead. People say that you don't really know someone until you live with them, but psychological abuse was something I hadn't put on the cards. It seems now that I was destined to be surrounded by forceful control freak men, whatever. First a very strict education where my own opinion was just not even considered, and then my boyfriend.

After some time, I literally escaped, taking just a bag of personal things with me and running for my life.

He was a police officer and seemed very kind, and I was very young and naive. After a while, the jealousy started to show, and I was not allowed even a female friend in the house for a coffee when I suggested continuing with piano lessons with a female teacher to keep him happy, all hell broke loose!

Once we started living together, his real personality came out, and I was constantly under control. We didn't do anything together like going to the theatre in Cambridge or going to a concert. We had nothing in common, nor did he want to participate in my interests. The only positive thing he did was give me permission to buy a dog, which kept me sane for a while. My beautiful black Labrador kept me company for months, and the long walks just the two of us were heaven. I made friends with another female police officer who had a golden retriever and was allowed to go walking with her and her dog; those were the highlights of my day and very precious moments. In fact, my friend Katy was also one of the few people who offered me a place to stay for a while when I fled from him.

Working in a police station in the beginning was hard and still very much a man's world. The new law had only recently allowed women to be officers and not just a sort of secretary, interviewing women and children or doing searches. It was a transition period and everything was new for everyone.

Even my first interview was pretty rocky and unexpected. It was with a senior male officer, obviously, who took great delight in telling me that I was absolutely nothing and a nobody because I was a woman and I had a lot to prove! He was obnoxious and basically on the verge of being offensive. Today, that sort of treatment would just not be tolerated, but in those days, I suppose they were normal, and I just listened and didn't retaliate. He put the fear of God into me, and I presume that was his idea, and that was just the beginning of my life as a doormat!

All seemed to go well in the beginning and I put in service for a couple of years in a small Fenland town, and my colleagues were respectful and friendly. I couldn't have wished for better, but then I met my future companion and transferred to Cambridge with him, and things started to go wrong.

After I fled, I still had my job at the station, but having left our home, word got around and my problems started in the office. The women would swarm around him with a "couldn't care less" attitude for what I was going through, nor did they show any respect or understanding. Such a strange world and an eye-opener of what was to come. He would come and check up on me in the office even after I had left our home and expect me to continue to do as I was told for the sake of appearances. When I finally started to stand up for myself, he became very nasty, and his male colleagues would take his side. It was very stressful, and I felt helpless. My friend Katy took me under her wing for a while, and a couple of other people were decent to me, but I realised that this situation could not go on and I must grow up and stop depending on others as they would get fed up with me.

Isn't it strange how, in times of trouble, you find out who your real friends are? In this case, his male colleagues all stuck together and made my life hell. They put me under so much pressure that I eventually had to leave my job.

In the beginning, they sent the police representative round to my house, and he tried to convince me to go back. There was no asking me how I felt or what the problems were. It was just trying to make me give in so everything could return to normal. If a relationship doesn't work, then why should I go back and waste my life?

It was the right decision for me and I wish I had been that decisive with other future problems.

One or two friends put me up and I was literally going from one friend to another for a time just to have a bed to sleep in. He changed the locks on my house and no one in the police force did anything to help. Never in a million years could I have imagined that the same story would repeat itself in the years to come, but in a different country and on a more catastrophic level! Given the situation, I felt I had nothing more to lose, and it was a now-or-never situation to make a fresh start. All those documentaries on TV make you think that perhaps there is something better, so let's give it a try. There was some sort of musical sound about the Italian language and during my period of being a bit of a hobo and shoved off from one place to another just to survive, Italy came to mind.

I obtained information by writing to different agencies and went off to London to an au pair agency to see what was available in Italy. I'd always wanted to learn another language, and what could be better than learning it on the spot, then maybe France with a couple of languages under my belt, the job opportunities should be quite good.

I've lost my home, I've lost my job, and I'm in complete disgrace with my family for being a failure, so what next? Ok, I have nothing more to lose. Why not go abroad? And so be it!

CHAPTER 3

The au pair agency vetted their clients and tried to find a family that would be a good match for the person requesting the position. My interview was with a pleasant English lady not much older than myself. Very petite with short blonde hair and of course very expensive Italian designer clothes. I suppose if she could afford an au pair, she must be very well off and, living in Italy, famous for its fashion, her look was not a surprise, but rather an admiration and the thought of who knows what's to come.

She talked to me about her life as an ex-model. Being so petite, she obviously wasn't doing the catwalks where the two-meter-tall girls were parading. I would say more of a facial model for makeup and hair, probably. Anyhow, she seemed quite nice and told me about her daughter of three that needed looking after. She assured me that she would do her duties as a mother and I was just to be a little bit of a help. I would have time off to go to school, have my own privacy and just a little pocket money as board and lodgings would be free. Being my first experience, and in fact, having no experience of anything at all, really, it seemed too good to be true. So we organised a date and flight, and I would be off to Italy for a new life.

I packed a big bag of essentials. Having lost my home and most of my belongings, I really didn't have much left, so I was leaving possibly for the rest of my life with one big bag. Thinking about it now, I don't know if I would do it again, but that was the first 26 years of my life, all in one big bag!

As I was leaving London, I thought I would stay with a girlfriend there so I would be nearer to the airport on the day, and I also hoped she would accompany me and see me off to say goodbye. No such luck; she had other things to do, and that was very sad. Many people travel for work, and getting a plane is like getting on a train and doing only a few kilometres, but it was absolutely daunting for me. Being a country girl and not having any city life experience made me think about how on earth I would cope in a foreign city not speaking the language. At 26 I still needed someone to hold my hand and was not capable of doing anything. Well, too late now. I've got myself into it. Let's see it through! I just kept telling myself that I had nothing more to lose, so I just got on with it, and that's what I did.

I said goodbye to my friend in London and went to the airport. So many new experiences. In fact, I think this was probably only the second time I had ever got on a plane, and my nerves were really playing up. Keep going, I told myself, it's only a couple of hours flight and then Ms Petite will be at the airport to pick you up and finally all the troubles will be left behind.

CHAPTER 4

I arrived at Linate airport and as promised, my new boss was waiting for me, and we went to get her car. We began our trip to the centre of Milan, where they lived. The air was hot and muggy, and the sky was grey and smoggy. The long road from the airport to get into the centre of Milan was the same, quite daunting. As we got nearer to the centre, the road on both sides became very oppressive with high buildings which were dirty and grey. It gave me a terrible, suffocating feeling, and I suddenly felt trapped. It was overwhelming and not a nice sensation at all.

The nearer we got, the more noise there was. At every traffic light, my boss took great delight in showing how Italian she had become by gesticulating with her fists at anybody who didn't get off the mark at the first hint of orange but instead, quite correctly, waited for the green light. I found it rather funny how everyone seemed to be in such a hurry, as though gaining those few seconds at the traffic lights was a matter of life and death. Even in the centre of London, they wait for the green and certainly don't start hooting and insulting the car in front of them for the slightest error or delay. Whatever land have I come to? And just how long am I going to last in such a place, and this is only my first day!

We finally got through the traffic and I could see us approaching Milan's Duomo, the big cathedral with its Italian gothic style and very overpowering. The building started in 1387 and took nearly six centuries to complete. It is the largest cathedral in the whole of Italy and the fifth largest in the world and very impressive. Even from a distance, I could see the famous "Madonnina," a baroque gilded bronze statue on the top of the main spire of the cathedral, which must be over 100 meters high.

Well, if this is anything to go by we must be going to one of the most expensive areas of Milan so can't wait to see my new boss' house!

We finally arrive having to get through tiny back streets to avoid the centre. We leave the car in an alleyway and walk into their residence.

First, the entrance took us into a huge courtyard, and an overwhelming historical abode suddenly faced me. Looking from the courtyard, the building was a horseshoe shape with large porches and arcades, which were quite impressive. On top of the arcade was a balcony following the shape all around and where the living quarters were. Big windows opened onto the balcony with typical Italian shutters on all of them. It reminded me a bit of pictures I had seen of Tuscany, but here we were in the centre of Milan. Once into their premises, it was surprisingly quiet and cut off from the noise of the city centre and yet we were only a five minutes walk from the cathedral. It really did seem like another world. It could even have been an old Monastery on first impressions and something you just wouldn't expect to discover in a busy city centre like Milan. Unfortunately, there were renovations going on all over the place, and it looked like they had probably just bought the place and were doing it up. There must be at least twenty rooms in the place and so big for a family of three, but there should be some room and privacy for me!

We climb the external stairs to enter into the living quarters and go through a labyrinth of rooms. Everything is having work done to it, so the actual living space is very limited, and I find myself in a dining room where I will have to sleep. On the sofa, that's great!!

So if we are going to eat here and at night I'm going to have to kip down, I'm going to have zero privacy. So much for honesty about what the situation was. Well, I'm here now, so will have to give it a try. She then introduces me to the little blonde girl, the spitting image of her mother. The little daughter started to make a scene almost immediately. She was a spoiled little brat and I thought things were not looking good here. It must be very nice to be so rich, but that doesn't mean there are excuses for not educating a little three-year-old madam who already thinks she is the queen of the city and can get away with anything. I try to make friends, and then later on, the husband comes home, and I make his acquaintance. A tall, striking young man with a beautiful tailored

Italian suit, of course, and surprisingly, not at all snob. In fact, he was very well-mannered and put me at ease, which is more than I can say for mother and child. He was a film director and obviously very successful judging by their house or, rather should I say, huge villa cum historical building.

His work took him all over the place, so it would be rare to see him at home.

We had dinner together in my bedroom/living room/dining room. A typical pasta dish with minute portions, as the wife obviously wanted to keep an eye on her figure. Appearances, as I later found out, are the most important thing in Milan. It is essential to show off even if you don't have the means to do it, although in this case, of course, money was evidently no problem. Having had a very strict education, I couldn't ask for another help, which would have been rude, so I went to bed with my stomach grumbling all night!

The next day, my job was to keep little Mirella occupied and play games together. She was a bossy little thing and used to getting her own way, which made her completely out of control.

She often had a bad temper and, one day, broke a beautiful vase, which I got blamed for. Being only three, I had hoped that I could put her to bed early. Most children in England have to go to bed at a certain time, and at least when I was little, there was no room for discussion. You just did as your parents told you. Unfortunately, this was not the case, and as I learned, children in Italy are very spoilt and stay up as long as they want. This meant that we had dinner together every evening at the time the adults ate, and she refused to go to bed before 11 p.m. The room in which we ate and played was, of course, my makeshift bedroom, which I had to turn into a bedroom when everyone else had finished doing what they were doing.

As the weeks went by, Mario, the husband, had some business in Venice, and it was decided that we would all go together, fantastic.

It was just over a three-hour drive by car, and of course, in a luxury car, the time passed quickly.

We left the car near the lagoon and got on the boat to get to the centre. It really was something out of a fairy tale. A floating city with its small alleyways, canals and bridges. The birthplace of Antonio Vivaldi, Piazza San Marco with its numerous amounts of pigeons and the very expensive chic coffee shops, arches and arcades, the smell of the water and of the damp old houses. Really something out of this world and quite correct when you hear people say that it is unique and there is nothing else like it anywhere else in the world. The view onto the Grand Canal and all the hustle and bustle was just incredible. The Venice carnival was also coming up so that will be very interesting.

We got to the apartment, and what an apartment. It must have been at least 300 square meters with beautiful blue carpets and we were basically on the lagoon itself. I have never seen anything like it.

In the next few days, Mario was on business, and his wife went with him, so I took the opportunity to discover the alleyways with Mirella.

St Mark's Basilica, the Doge's Palace, watching the gondoliers on the Gran Canal in their pretty little sailors costumes was all quite breathtaking. We would meet up in the evenings for dinner, and again, I learned more about how things work. Venice does have a lot of touristy restaurants and also a McDonald's, which is not at all in keeping with such a historical place by the way. In any case, I was told to always avoid tourist cuisine even if it does cost less. If you don't know anyone who lives there, then always find and ask one of the locals where he goes to eat and what he can recommend. In that way you have quality and taste the real thing. Italians are very attached to their eating habits; after appearances, I would say it's one of their top lists. Best food best restaurants, be seen in the "in" places. Heavens, is this really so important in life? I think Mario must be well known here because of his work, and he certainly knew his way around. After five minutes in these tiny dark alleyways, I would have been completely lost even with a map. We all went to a very nice restaurant and I had an evening eating typical food and living how the other half lives for a couple of hours.

Our few days in Venice came very quickly to an end and back we were in Milan to the usual everyday life.

I wasn't given much free time at all, contrary to what I had been told, and having no written contract, there wasn't much I could do. I tried to discover Milan's centre with little time, but this job just wasn't for me. On one of my discovery expeditions, I met a very nice young lady from Holland who was also an au pair, and I explained my situation to her. She was very helpful and told me that friends of the family where she was working were looking for an au pair and they would certainly be more honest about my chores than my present boss. She made a quick phone call, and voilà I had an interview.

CHAPTER 5

This family were in a modern apartment in a completely different neighbourhood. This time, I found myself in an area called Porta Ticinese. This area had medieval walls and a city gate, hence the name "Porta Ticinese," porta meaning gate or door. This name is both the name of the gate and the area. Milan is made up of zones and each of these areas has a name which distinguishes it. The medieval gate is one of the few remnants of the medieval 12th-century walls that are, in fact, still in place. Again very strange to see something like this in the middle of the city. This particular area, I found out had quite a lot of history.

The current location of the gate (in a plaza that is now called "Piazzale XIV Maggio") was established during the Spanish rule in the 16th century. In the early 19th century, most Spanish gates were demolished and replaced with new structures meant to serve as toll gates. This was also the case with Porta Ticinese.

I found out that this particular district was part of the Navigli area. The Navigli were a system of canals running through Milan, five in total. They are derelict and unnavigable today, although Naviglio Grande seemed to be quite an attraction for tourists and locals with its floating restaurants and walks along the canal where you could pop into a local jazz club or for a beer, not really like walking along by the Thames and seeing the London Eye as everything was in such smaller proportions but something certainly different and an oldy worldly feeling.

Anyway, this was going to be my new district for a while.

My new family had bought two apartments, knocked them into one, and made a very nice large apartment out of it with modern, good taste and I actually had my own bedroom this time. Their only son was 8, and he too, was rather obnoxious. Is this how all Italian children are I thought? This time, I had to help out in the house and didn't have so much to do with the child so things looked a bit brighter. I just had to get him his tea daily and do some cleaning, which suited me better. The family consisted of the husband, some sort of import export dealer in what I never knew, and the wife and mother-in-law, who shared an exclusive lingerie shop in the centre of Milan. They were very nice people and treated me very well. I had much more free time and also went to visit them in their shop. Their lingerie range was very exclusive, and they said that as I was working for them, I could have a big discount if I wanted to buy anything. One of their main brands in particular was my favorite but you could pay as much as 100 euros just for a pair of knickers! I don't think that will happen on my babysitter wage somehow!

With my free time I walked a lot and got to know the centre of the city. I even managed to get inside La Scala theatre once and have a quick peep.

I think it was obvious that I was a foreigner as I got stopped many times on my walks by lads asking if I would like a coffee. It was quite flattering, and they certainly weren't shy! Something that I was not at all used to in England, where everyone seems to go about their own business, and nobody notices anyone around them. I met quite a few people this way, and it was rather a nice little social life in the beginning.

I discovered Via della Spiga, one of the very elite streets just off the centre where all the famous fashion brands were to be found and of course only affordable to the rich. A very pleasant and quiet street, and all the shop windows were a feast to the eyes. From leather goods to clothes and shoes and the very tempting "pasticcerie," the bakery shops where you could buy tiny little bite-size cakes. These are a tradition for Italians. They will buy a tray to take to guests when invited to dinner or for some special occasion. Then, of course, every 10 meters, there was a bar of some kind where you could simply have an espresso coffee and a brioche or have a quick lunch of salad or a panino, a filled roll of ham and cheese or salad. These bars are very popular with office workers who have very little time and just pop in for a snack on a half-hour lunch break.

CHAPTER 6

Time went by, and the summer holiday period came around. My family had a holiday home on the island of Elba, and this is where they went every summer. So we packed our things and prepared for a month of seaside life on the third largest island in Italy.

We had to get a tiny plane to actually get us onto the island, which I didn't like very much. I don't like flying and on a plane so small you can feel even the slightest bit of wind, but fortunately it was a nice day and not very long on the plane and I made it without being sick!

They had a nice house, not really very big but pleasant and with a huge courtyard where you could sit and look at the sea and eat outside. It was very hot being August, but with the sea breeze, it was bearable. The walks along the seafront were very nice and so many little shops of all sorts made it very interesting.

We would eat out in the evenings along by the seafront, and there would always be a huge "tavolata," which literally means table. Still, the Italians use it to describe a load of friends and family getting together. It seemed like half of Milan had transferred to the island for their holidays as although there were some tourists, everybody seemed to know everybody, and there were all sorts of friends and neighbours that we would bump into. My family would stop and chat or organise to see them later on for an "aperitivo" or for dinner later in one of the restaurants.

That was a weird sensation for me as I had always thought that the whole idea of a holiday was to actually get away from people you know and have a real break. But here, it is quite the opposite. You basically carry on with your life with the same family and friends but in a different place. Oh well, if that pleases them!

My family also had a small fishing boat and their son loved to go out on that. I did have a lot of free time while they went out together, so rather than work it was a holiday for me and all paid for too. I had many walks along the seafront and felt very lucky at that time. Although the family were upper class and had many friends and acquaintances of the same standing, the people I met were all very pleasant and didn't make me feel uneasy. That is certainly a pleasant turnaround after the last family I was with.

My family all spoke English, and although they knew I was trying to learn Italian, they would revert to English if they thought I didn't understand. In fact, going out alone was good for my learning practice, particularly when I was sent out to do the shopping for them at the supermarket or on other errands, as I was thrown in at the deep end and had to get on with it. This really is one of the best ways to learn more quickly and although a little overwhelming at first, I soon came to appreciate doing errands while improving my language skills.

During one of our evenings of eating out, some other family friends were at the table, including a friend's daughter.

Diana was a girl of my own age, and her English was quite good, so we could converse during dinner and be good friends during the month on the island. She lived with her mother in an apartment in a different area of Milan to my family but within easy distance using public transport. So we organised a get-together after the holidays and promised that we would keep in touch.

Little did I know that in the near future, my life would be filled with problems, evil and nastiness, and so I can now look back on this particular moment in time with fond memories filled with kind and friendly people always making themselves available to help, particularly Diana who would be a big part of my life for the next couple of years.

Our month on Isola d'Elba came to a close, and sadly, we had to go back to the grim, grey, smoggy, dirty, ugly hustle and bustle of Milan!

We got back to the city just before the end of August, and much to my surprise I found a deserted city, almost unrecognisable. The shops were closed, there was hardly anyone on the streets and very little traffic.

What is going on? I ask myself. Now I have to search for a supermarket that is actually open. Everyone is still on holiday, and it literally is from the 1st till the 31st of August. No bread shops open, the chemists take turns to be on duty and to find one you may have to walk miles.

My family explained that it was a tradition here, and the Breda factory, where mainly southern Italians worked, would close down for the whole month so they could go down south to be with their families. As a consequence, everything else closed down, as there was very little trade. In fact the tourists that came during this month were very disappointed finding a deserted city. Nowadays, things are more efficient as the factory has closed and offices and factories, to make ends meet, have to work in a more European style and so try to keep things open, making their employees take turns for holiday periods so that even if there is a skeleton staff places have to remain open. You can still perceive the difference in August even now if you are unfortunate enough to have to stay in the city during the summer. Still, at least some shops are open and the supermarkets are always open which gives the elderly the possibility of getting away from the terrible heat and humidity. They pass their days in the shopping centres where there is good air conditioning. This is in fact, another reason why people try to get away to a different climate. The weather is really unbearable during this period, with a high humidity rate and terrible heat. Hence, anyone who can afford air conditioning has it installed, as it really is a must. After a few days, everything returned to normal, and we did our usual chores.

Most well-off families here have both a summer holiday home and a winter one and as the weeks went by, it was time for another in-between holiday break before the winter.

Well, I think I could get used to this! We were going to the sea again, but this time in Liguria, they had another house by the sea. Even in winter in this area, the climate was always milder, and we could get away from the colder, damp weather of the city for a long weekend. The weather really was beautiful and the beaches were clean and sandy rather than pebbly, lovely for walking barefoot.

During our weekend, we went on a trip to Portofino. This was a tiny fishing town, very small and with an air of tranquillity. The place was so small in fact that we had to leave the car at quite a distance and we walked into the town. There were little streets leading up from the harbour and very expensive boutiques, and getting into the Piazzetta by the harbour, I found many cafes and restaurants, a wonderful atmosphere to sit down and have a drink and just watch the people go by and the boats going in and out. My goodness, was this an exclusive place? This was for the very rich yachting jet set. Just seeing how people were dressed, and the beautiful yachts in the harbour made my eyes goggle. Walking the lanes and coming across the yachting boutiques, jewellery shops, and art galleries was a world that I had never seen. This little town was a jewel and quite breathtaking in its beauty. I could see why so many tourists came here. It really was like a fairytale.

The time went quickly and we were soon back in the city waiting for the Christmas period to come along and another holiday!

CHAPTER 7

The usual days went by with work and errands, a bit of cleaning and cooking and the colder weather set in. The atmosphere was so damp in this area that your body perceived the temperature as being even colder. It was a weird feeling; the dampness seemed to get right into my bones. No wonder people can leave the city as often as possible. With the smog and the humidity, it is not a healthy climate.

This time, of course, we would be having a real winter holiday, but whether my family prefer the sea and warmth in the winter or a proper winter holiday remains to be seen.

I didn't possess many clothes and I couldn't buy much on the pocket money I was given, so I was never prepared for the holidays, be it summer or winter. My family told me not to worry and that they would be able to lend me the necessary as it would be very cold where we were going.

We set out for the mountains and were going to yet another of their holiday homes. This time, it was Madonna di Campiglio, a village and ski resort in the northeast of Italy in the Alps. This would be a first for me having never ever been to a mountain area in my life. We were going to be 1,500 meters above sea level, so not a really exaggerated height, but still going to be very cold. There were several ski tracks, some of which reached a higher 2,600 meters, and I can only imagine how cold that would be! I was told that at night, we could expect temperatures of minus 20 in the area that we were going to, so thank goodness my family had lent me some warm clothes!

They had a nice little mountain house, which was thankfully well-heated, and the next day, we would be going for a walk and discovering the centre. There were also lots of public footpaths and walks on nature trails for those who didn't ski, as in my case.

Here in the mountains, as had happened on our summer holiday, we bumped into many people from Milan, and my family met up with friends from the city who were also on vacation. Their friends were a very nice couple who we arranged to go trekking with the next day. It was so cold, and the right clothes were necessary. They lent me a pair of moon boots, which were wonderful. It made walking in the snow so much easier, and they were so warm, just what I needed.

We had a very nice week with lots of nature trail walks, aperitifs late afternoon with friends in the snowy centre and again I was made welcome and had a pleasant time. Having had such a sheltered life in England, absolutely everything was new to me, and my first year in Italy was a big discovery.

Our winter holiday ended, and we had to return to the city's cold and dampness. It was strange how in the mountains where the temperature was really low, but with a dry cold, it was easier to resist. Here in the city, it was probably 20 degrees warmer, and yet I felt colder here than in the mountains!

Back in the city, I caught up with my new friend Diana and we often met up for a coffee or a walk in the city. She often invited me for lunch in her apartment, where she lived with her mother, and we got talking about what I should do in the future.

My Italian was still not very good at all. So she helped me by reading the advertisements in the newspaper just to see what could be available for an English speaking person with not really any work experience. My job in the police force wasn't going to help but she said that there were a lot of international companies in Milan where my English would be useful even though I couldn't yet speak Italian properly.

During my walks of the area on my time off I had discovered a "gelateria," an ice-cream parlour where they made their own delicious Italian ice creams and they were looking for help in the evenings. As my family gave me a lot of time off I asked if I could apply as the money would be useful. They made no objections, and strangely enough, the owner took me on without me having good knowledge of the language. Most people point to the flavours they want, so I ought to be able to handle it. Besides, being thrown in at the deep end would help me to learn the language more quickly in a working environment.

The gelateria wasn't too far from my family, so I could walk to work in the evenings. There wasn't a lot to do in the winter, of course, as ice creams are more of a summer delight, but as the warmer weather started again, we were rushed off our feet, and the little shop was very popular. It was also a nice way to meet people, and little by little, I managed to chat with customers, and my Italian started to improve.

The gelateria also had a bar on the other side of the shop where people would come in for an espresso, and this part was run by a barista who seemed to take me under his wing for some reason. During my season there I was asked out quite a bit, which shocked me, not being used to so much attention. I think it was the novelty of a "straniera," a foreigner, being in the shop more than anything else, and one young man in particular who was a doctor was very interesting. He was a regular customer, and I decided to accept his invitation to go out for coffee together.

However, the next time he came in he seemed to be embarrassed and didn't mention the invite again. I couldn't understand why. Of course, he could have changed his mind but he seemed to be sincere and not the sort of person to make fun of others. I don't remember how the conversation came about, but one day, the owner of the shop said that I was so naïve that I couldn't see what was happening in front of me and that his barista had become very possessive and every time a man looked at me he would frighten them off and tell them that I was his property! I couldn't believe it. I had never given him the impression that I was interested in him, so why did he decide to organise my life? This went on for quite a while, and I decided that I couldn't work in that sort of atmosphere and under the control of someone who had no business to do so. It was quite a good working experience, however, and made me realise that perhaps I should now look for a job which would be more in keeping with something I wanted in the future.

I told Diana that the time had come to branch out and become independent, so we started job hunting and writing CVs. I told my family about my decision, and we left on very friendly terms.

CHAPTER 8

Diana was right about the boom for English speaking people. Even with no experience I soon found a job as a receptionist in a very prestigious law firm right in the centre of Milan.

Now, I needed a place to stay. Diana said she knew someone who had a little flat that he used to bring his lady friends to, but as at the moment he was single, I could rent it for a while.

She introduced me to her acquaintance and we went to look at the flat. It was right in the heart of the Navigli and fairly easy to get into town for my new job. It was a tiny attic with just one window on the roof. All open space, and a very tiny space at that. It had one bed, a TV, a tiny shower and an "angolo cottura," which literally means cooking corner. It was just that! The bare essentials but at a good price and would do for now. With the summer coming and the flat being on the riverside, the damp heat and the mosquitos were unbearable, but for the moment, I would have to put up with it.

I was accepted into the law firm on a very basic wage, and my job was to deal with English-speaking clients. The firm had a lot of American clients, and when Italians were in the studio, there was always someone from the accounts department around to help me out with the language problem. The accounts department was next to my reception area, and they were all very kind and helpful during my three years with this firm. My Italian improved considerably as they chatted to me a lot putting my mistakes right and having a good laugh when I got my phrases wrong and a totally different meaning came out from what I actually wanted to say. One day, we were talking about recipes and cooking and how to make a good broth. I was trying to say what sort of meat "carne" I used to make a broth, but I said "cane" instead, which means a dog" so I was basically saying that I made my broths with dog meat, so you can imagine the laughs that were heard right to the end of the studio! I didn't make that mistake again!

My rent was half my wage, so I had to be very careful in managing my budget. It wasn't easy, and I couldn't afford a social life. Thankfully, Diana was always available, and having a friend just to do simple things without spending was nice. Before getting to the office in the morning, everyone used to pop into the bar for a coffee before work; that was about all I could afford. These bars are such social areas and meeting places. I got to know so many people in this way and got a lot of invites but had to decline due to my budget. It was embarrassing to say that I couldn't afford a social life and, so, usually made something feasible. Some of the guys realised the situation and said they were very happy to offer but I just couldn't bring myself to take advantage. Morning breakfast of Cappucino and brioche, then the morning break for an espresso. These places are just humming with activity, office workers and shoppers of all sorts and the more, the merrier.

I started learning my new job and got into the swing of things. In the meantime the flat owner was also very nice and invited me for a panino for lunch at the weekend. He knew I was on a very tight budget and had only enough to eat simply, and I thought that his invites were very kind. Our weekend lunch got to be a habit, and although I could never see myself getting involved sentimentally, he was quite good company. But, as all good things come to an end, it seems, so did this. On one of our lunches, he suddenly said that he certainly wasn't doing this out of the goodness of his heart and all debts should be paid so therefore, he expected me to start sleeping with him. Miss naïve that I am, I was completely shocked and didn't see that coming at all! Whenever I was going to learn to see through people and not always see only the good in them. I thanked him for the lunch and told him quite politely that this was never going to happen.

I went to work the next day, and when I got home in the evening, I found that someone had been in the flat. Of course, the owner had a spare set of keys; this was normal, but once a place had been rented out, they should not let themselves in without asking permission. He had taken the TV and everything else out of the place and a note saying that the rent had gone up. The price he was asking was the whole sum of my wage. What a pig. I couldn't obviously stay in such a similar situation. I told Diana about it and said I needed somewhere to stay. She was furious with him and she herself hadn't expected such behaviour from him so I felt a little consoled in that I wasn't the only one to have been fooled.

CHAPTER 9

At this time, house prices were very low, and we considered the fact that paying a mortgage would be the same as paying rent, and perhaps it was something we should look into.

In the law firm, there was a continual coming and going of documents delivered and picked up by a service called "Pony Express." They were lads on motorbikes or with small vans according to the packets or letters being delivered between one law firm and another. I got talking to one of the lads who said he could help me find a small flat at a good price and we organised a meeting for that coming weekend.

On my limited wage, we had to look at very small apartments and, in the end, found something cheap and near to a bus stop to get to work. The flat was very run down and needed a lot of doing, hence its price. It had one tiny bedroom, a kitchen and a minute bathroom, but for me on my own could be a start. My friend said he was good at doing things up and not to worry about a few renovations as he had plans and could give me a hand. The boss in the accounting department worked out a payment plan that would not take the whole of my wage away, and we decided to go for it.

Everything seemed to go ahead as planned and then just as I had hoped, things changed yet again. He was from Sicily and had been promised marriage to a girl from the area. I actually didn't think that sort of thing still existed. However, he explained that she was expecting and, therefore, the wedding would have to be sooner than planned and that he would be moving back to Sicily. That's brilliant, I thought. We haven't even started on the work in the house, and I have nowhere to live.

At my workplace, they helped me find a company that would do the place up in a very basic way, and I could pay a bit at a time. I was lent a camp bed and had no other choice but to live for a few months in this way. At least I had a roof over my head and hopefully, it would be an investment for the future. The workers, however, kept asking for more money as they went along and my tiny wage was not enough, so I will just have to look for an extra job. With me speaking English, I often got requests for help, so I took on some teaching in the evenings. That still wasn't enough, so I had to look for something else. I found an early morning cleaning job, making my day tough. I was up a 6 a.m. to do a couple of hours cleaning, then off to the office, after which to my private teaching job, getting home about midnight, and still I was only just making ends meet. I spoke to my colleagues who had found the workers for me and said they were conning me and would have a word with them. They said that because I was foreign and female, this was quite the norm for people to be taken advantage of. Thankfully, they put things straight for me, and the company had to accept that I had already paid enough. If they weren't happy, they would be getting a complaint letter from the law firm, and I would be suing them, so that shut them up finally.

I carried on with my long days of work for a couple of years due to necessity, and the area in which I was living certainly wasn't one of the most tranquil spots.

One evening, I was waiting for the bus late at night, as usual, after my English class. The bus stop was on a busy road, which was rather well-known as a pick-up place for men looking for "young ladies of the night."

Although I was dressed in a suit after my day's work and evidently not one of these ladies, I can't remember how long cars would stop, and men would offer me money. Some of the guys were the typical "dirty old men" type and quite honestly disgusted me. Still, some, much to my surprise, were young, good-looking guys, and I couldn't for the life of me understand why they should need company when I'm sure they would have no difficulty finding a girlfriend with their good looks. Needless to say, I looked the other way and pretended they were not there, and thankfully, no one insisted or got rough. Even though it was a well-known area for this sort of thing, never once did I see a police car pass by and do a routine check. Moreover, it was a busy road with lots of offices and not what I would have considered your usual out-of-the-way hidden spot. In any case, people just got on with their "business," and the police obviously just turned a blind eye. I had to get used to this way of life and learnt to keep my eyes down and pretend nothing was happening and usually I was left in peace. On one of these eventful evenings, there were a bunch of people at the bus stop, more than usual, making me feel a little more safe.

Quite the contrary as it happened, as all of a sudden a young man suddenly unbuttoned his raincoat for all the world to see what was underneath! And that was, of course, absolutely nothing! The man was completely naked and not a pretty sight. It was quite funny after the shock as his raincoat was a perfect copy of the actor Lieutenant Colombo. Here in Italy, the television series has been running for years, and they call this rather particular American police officer "Tenente Colombo," famous for his dirty raincoat in all seasons and his unassuming presence. This guy could have been a younger version. The handful of people at the bus stop didn't even seem to be surprised. Everyone just pretended nothing was happening, and nobody came to my defence to make him stop. Given that he was preying on me in particular, as he was standing right in front of me and being quite a pain in the neck, I would have thought that at least somebody would have given me a hand getting rid of him, but no such thing. He was so insistent and kept following me when I tried to get out of his reach, so in the end, out of desperation, I scuttled off and decided to walk a couple of miles home to get away from him!

CHAPTER 10

Time went by, and I managed to get out now and again putting what I could out of my pittance of a wage aside and go visiting. I went back to Liguria, where I had been with my last family, but this time, I visited the "Cinque Terre." It's a portion of the coast on the Italian Riviera and means "five lands." It comprises five villages and one can walk a very rugged coastline from one village to the next. I managed to do this walking trail, the "sentiero azzurro," where there is no development and some parts were quite strenuous but such beautiful views. Definitely well worth doing.

I got the train back to Milan and talked to a girl in the same carriage who was also returning to the central station. She lived not far away from me and we decided to keep in touch once back in Milan. We met up quite a few times, and I was introduced to her group of friends. Everyone seems to go out in big groups here, which makes it fun. We would go out for a pizza or to a gelateria after dinner, particularly on weekends. We sometimes sat around a table till 2 in the morning. This little group was going to be my downfall. Little did I know that one of her friends, who was later to be my husband, would turn out to be a liar, a con man and a real badass!

During this time I had met quite a few people and one girl called Lucinda, just like me, became a good friend. She invited me quite often to her place, and her English was perfect, so we enjoyed some good conversations. When I had any problems, she always knew someone who could help. I needed a bit of electrical work doing in the flat and she sent a friend of hers over. He had to bash in a bit of wall where the plug was and then didn't have the right materials with him to finish the job so he decided to leave it and come back the next day. By this time, it was getting dark, and so when the neighbours came back and switched on their lights, I saw, to my horror, that the handyman had bashed the wall right through to their apartment! The hole was in my bedroom, and as it was very late when the two lads who were my neighbours got back, the light in their flat suddenly woke me up, and I saw two pairs of eyes staring at me in bed and a hole big enough for them to climb through!

So much for being a handyman. Thankfully, they weren't cross, and I said I'd get it fixed the next day. After the initial fright I put some cardboard over the hole for some privacy but didn't get back to sleep at all. They were a pretty rough couple, and I certainly couldn't afford to upset them. However, I called my friend the next day and explained what had happened to her. She sent her handyman friend immediately, and we got the situation back under control.

The walls in these flats are like paper, and you can hear everything that goes on. I'd never lived in a flat as in the countryside in England we all lived in a house or a bungalow so hearing every word the neighbours speak is not a nice feeling. My neighbours also had some sort of trafficking in what was certainly illegal substances, and there was always a coming and going at all hours of the night. They were actually quite friendly to me, and as long as I minded my own business, I never had any trouble with them. It's not the sort of environment I would have chosen to be on my own, but that is another problem of not speaking the language and getting a feel of the area before you buy somewhere!

Living in a condominium was a first for me, like living in a rabbit hutch. It was so oppressive and had zero privacy. So many rules and regulations that I was supposed to respect but that nobody else did. I had a minute balcony outside my bedroom and was in the habit of putting my washing out before going to work. Given the very limited space in the flat, my balcony was an extra and very useful. I would get home from work, find my washing dirty, and wash it all over again. One day, I saw why. I was doing the cleaning in the bedroom at the weekend and a flurry of dirt came falling onto the balcony. Low and behold, the upstairs neighbours were shaking their dirty tablecloth and everything else, and of course, it was landing on my property and on my clean washing. Mystery resolved, I asked them if they would please stop doing this as it was also one of the regulations that was supposed to be respected. They just laughed and carried on as before. I couldn't put my washing out again but at least I didn't waste electricity having to do a double wash of the same things.

This continued going on and on, and so in the end, out of frustration, I collected their dirt from my balcony, went upstairs to their apartment, and very happily emptied the bag of their dirt all over their entrance. Why is it that I have to come down to this level to make myself understood? You can't reason with these people. They just looked at me in wonder as though I was a Martian, and I did ask nicely. This obviously is not the way things work here. Another lesson learnt.

CHAPTER 11

As time went by, my Italian was improving, and my wage as a receptionist was still so low that I decided it was time to look for something a little more challenging. This time, I was able to search the newspapers for myself and write my own CV. I had a few interviews but in the end I managed to find a new job just around the corner from the law firm thanks to a colleague who put me in touch with the company. She had a friend in an international firm with headquarters in London and they needed someone as a PA with good English. I loved this job and although the hours were long, it didn't bother me. There were only four of us in this representative office plus a lady boss. She was young, spoke four languages and very career orientated. She wasn't at all bossy however, and we got on very well.

I had kept in touch with the girl I had met on the train and during one of our outings, she had introduced me to Fabrizio. He was a trainee electrician and seemed very kind. He had asked me out several times, and I think being on my own and having to face so many problems, meeting him took some weight off me, and I accepted. It was a relief to be able to get things fixed, and I noticed that when a man took charge of things everything miraculously got done. It was probably this that blinded me, as looking back, we had absolutely nothing in common, and so it must have been his kind approach that put me off guard.

I was so naïve and still wasn't really into understanding how things worked here, so when we went out with the whole group of friends, I thought it was normal. Never did we have a romantic evening together or a meal, just the two of us. All his friends were always there tagging along whatever. I suppose having missed out a lot on a social life I saw this as an opportunity to recuperate a bit of lost time. I was living like a teenager again, which I had definitely missed out on and was now having a good time.

We had a lot of fun doing the usual things kids do: having an ice cream on weekends or going to the bars for a beer. One of his friends had a really run-down rented house in the mountains, so we would often organise a weekend to go up picking mushrooms in the woods or just going for a coffee in the local bar and then preparing a bowl of pasta in the evening and just generally hanging out. For weekends in the winter, a whole group of us would get together, sometimes even as many as a dozen of us. It was crazy trying to kip down in the evenings with not enough beds for all of us. With no heating, the first job was to light a fire, and the living room was the only place to keep warm with below-zero temperatures outside. Each group had its job to do like collecting wood for the fire, then a group would have to face the cold in the kitchen and get the pan on for the pasta. Others would set the table, and others would just drink and do nothing. One of the popular super alcoholic drinks was Grappa. This was exceptionally strong but did keep you warm. Needless to say, many of the lads overdid the grappa drinking and were absolutely hopeless in helping with any other chores needed! We were all in our 30s at the time, but it seemed like we were teenagers without a care in the world, so we carried on for another couple of years in the same way.

One of Fabrizio's friends had started to frequent the Oktober Fest, the beer festival in Munich. A couple would take him along in a camper, and they had a fantastic time. He suggested that our group could do the same thing. We had many years going to the Oktober Fest and basically, I was taken along to translate as Fabrizio would have been quite happy being just with his friends. A clue that I should have seen right from the beginning as to what our future lives would be. In any case, I did have a lot of fun and travelled round Germany for a few years, appreciating the courtesy and the respect from the Germans that was missing in Italy.

CHAPTER 12

In the meantime, he said we should get married. I still can't remember to this day anything about the proposal, so that's how memorable it was! I do remember saying, however that as I wasn't a young girl anymore, for me, it would be better to live together as I didn't see any point in getting married. When he said that his mother would never approve of such a thing, it should have been once again an alarm bell for me, but I always seemed to give the benefit of the doubt and went ahead.

Little did I know that "la famiglia è sacra," the "family is sacred" tradition over here, would be taken literally and be my downfall in years to come.

Apparently, before you are officially engaged, you have to be introduced to the family otherwise, it's not valid and hence an introduction to them all. Once you step inside the family's four walls, there is no going back or at least it is very difficult.

I was taken to their small apartment, a one bedroomed rabbit hutch like everywhere else in the city, and where the two sons growing up kipped down in the living room on a sofa bed. The father was a factory worker, and the mother was a housewife. Their flat was rented, and they had been there for about thirty years since they both came up from the south of Italy to find work. The father came up north at a time when, in the South, in the small town where he was born, most people were agricultural workers, and there were very few possibilities of doing anything else if not to work on the land. The father was a very ordinary and pleasant person and made me welcome but the mother, a wiry little thing that reminded me of a witch, started to pick on me immediately. The fact that I was a foreigner did not go down very well at all, but as her son seemed intent on marrying me, she decided that a warning was all she could do. I still remember her words as though they were yesterday. She got up on her high horse and told me in an awful commanding voice that the fact that I was taking her son away was already bad enough and, in her opinion, a huge injustice towards her. Still, if I ever dared to even think about going back to England with him then I would be a dead person! Well, this is a great beginning, I thought to myself. I didn't really take it too seriously, however, as this was the first time I had been introduced to an Italian family, and I didn't want to believe that this was the norm.

The lecture still hadn't finished with her death threat. As if that wasn't enough, she then explained how things work in Italy according to her house rules and that I must obey or else……!

Incredible, just what does she want this awful witch? She then went on to explain that sons, not daughters, but only sons, are the "bastone della vecchiaia." This literally means the walking stick for old age. She had not had children for the love of it, oh no, on the contrary, solely for her selfish gains, and that is having the security of being looked after now and in her old age, and no-one should dare discuss her decisions or get in her way. My goodness, please let me get out of here before I throw a wobbly!

During this comedy, his father was there. He seemed to be a very nice, placid, normal man, totally the opposite of his wife. He tried his best to make me feel welcome and play down his wife's awful start. He would laugh about her behaviour and say that he would have been better off in prison rather than marrying her, and if he had been sent to prison after all this time, he would have been out now and a free man! Although he tried to make a joke of it, I could see that there was certainly some truth in what he was saying. Poor man, I did not envy him.

As it was an official introduction to the family, both his brother and sister-in-law were also there.

The sister-in-law Marisa was a small, rather overweight woman from Sicily and evidently the boss. Her husband, Faby's brother, was a huge, wimpy piece of lard and gave me the shivers. He just sat in a corner and didn't say a word. Marisa, on the other hand, wouldn't stop talking, and even if you paid her, she had no switch-off button, and my head was exploding with her stupid chit-chat.

Between the nasty mother and the bossy sister-in-law, it was quite a feat to remain in my right mind.

My duty done, we left, and after such an experience I mentioned once again to Faby that at this stage we should live together and see how things go, particularly having just had a taste of a very nasty, wicked witch. However, yet again I was told that mummy wouldn't approve it and we would have to wait for the wedding.

We went to the town hall to see how to go about things, but as I was not a Catholic, I was told things would be somewhat difficult. So much for freedom of choice regarding one's personal religion, I thought to myself. This was a Catholic country, and I had been brought up as a Protestant and had no intention of changing my own religion. I was in Italy and therefore had to abide by their rules, of course, but being a Protestant did no harm to anyone, and in any case, I think I was doing enough for Faby and his family just by agreeing to get married.

CHAPTER 13

I went to the more important, main town hall in Milan and also to the diocese to ask for information. To my disgust, I was treated with great snobbery by the priest, who informed me that I would have to change my religion to be accepted here. It was very humiliating to be treated not only as an outsider but almost like a criminal. I certainly didn't expect that sort of behaviour from a priest, and I think he could at least have taken the time to be civil and maybe looked into the situation for various solutions. I left feeling very down and went home to give an account of the situation to Faby.

I suggested that we just have a civil ceremony which would be simpler and also less expensive. After all, my wage wasn't that high, and his family was obviously very poor. Yet again, my suggestion was treated with horror as there would certainly be repercussions if mother couldn't see her son marry in a real church. So, how to go about this without having to change my religion and keep mother happy? After many phone calls and going half way round Milan to different churches, I found a solution. We would have to go to England and get married officially in the town hall registry office, then have the marriage certificate legally translated, after which one of the few, if not the only protestant church in Milan, could do a service for us which would seem to all intents and purposes a proper wedding. Although we would already be officially married with the English ceremony, the church service in Milan would be just that, a religious service and not a legal wedding, but to all appearances, that would be the case, and mother would be none the wiser!

We had to be residents in England for three weeks at least before the civil ceremony could be officiated, so we had to work it round the holiday period in Italy, where Faby would not be working for the whole month of August. Faby would not be working. We stayed with my parents using their address as our UK residency which gave us in the fourth week just the time to have the civil ceremony. This done, we had lunch out in St. Ives in an Italian restaurant to celebrate and to make Fabrizio feel a little more at home.

The documents then had to be sent to the Consulate and await translation. This being done, the bands had to go up for a few weeks in the town hall in Milan before the marriage was officially accepted in Italy.

Before going to England, we tried to get a date for our church service, but it was so full that we were told we would have to wait till May the next year for this blessed service. There was no other choice and we booked the church on the first available date possible. The long wait was also due to the fact that one of his cousins, who owned a bakery shop, had his only day off on a Monday and insisted very strongly that the church service be on a Monday so he could come. This meant that everyone else would have to take a day off work and I didn't find that very correct. This guy was mother's favorite nephew and therefore, there was no discussion in the matter. As usual, what mummy wants, mummy gets! The service would have to be on a Monday to accommodate him, and others would have to get time off work if they wanted to come, and that was the end of it.

Our one-month holiday and civil wedding ended, and we got our flight back to Milan, ready to start a new life. Just imagine my surprise when Fabrizio returned to his mother's on arrival and didn't come home with me. I asked what was happening, and he replied that his mother had not permitted him to live with me because she hadn't seen him in church yet. But we are officially married, I told him, and it's about time you stood up to her. My goodness, if she is going to bully him like this things have got to be sorted out immediately. He obviously hasn't the guts to speak to her, so I will have to do it. I went round and explained that we were actually married, and she had no right to interfere. Nothing doing, she had one of her usual theatrical fits with crocodile tears, raving and ranting about how I had taken her son away and that until he was married in church nothing else for her was valid. Fabrizio just stood there like a wimp with his head hanging down, a complete dummy. This was the moment in which I should have had the marriage annulled and another of those moments that when I look back I think I'm the dummy for not having done so. I had to wait nearly a year after our marriage to actually live under the same roof with my own husband, and I stupidly waited for him.

The month of May was fast approaching with the farce of a fake wedding in church. I was told that we were to have lunch for the guests after the ceremony and we should also get on with ordering the "bomboniere." Apparently, all wedding guests have to receive a present to thank them for coming to the wedding. Not only do guests receive "confetti" during the celebration lunch, but they also receive "Bomboniere" which are small gifts. These gifts can be anything from a small porcelain bowl to crystal vases, according to your budget. You spend as much as you want, and the bigger the gift the better impression you give. The "confetti" is sugar almonds and not the coloured paper that you would throw over the bride and groom as you do in England. Although having the same name, the Italian "confetti" is part of the wedding tradition and is usually in small net bags attached to the bigger "Bomboniere" wedding gift. So, just how am I supposed to pay for all this on my wage I asked myself. I asked Fabrizio if we could keep costs down as I really couldn't afford to stick to all these traditions, and I also asked him to keep the guest list down. I still had to buy an outfit for the occasion and flowers as it was going to be in church.

Yet again, he couldn't make his mother see sense as, of course, she wanted to show off. Her reply was that she would pay for her guests and choose the "confetti" and "Bomboniere" for her side of the family. Who I invited was my affair, and I would have to pay for my side. Thanks a lot, I thought. Not happy with taking things into her own hands as far as invites are concerned she also informed me that in this family I would only be accepted if I dressed in white and what is more a "proper" wedding dress of HER choice!!! Really! Can this get any worse, and in what language do I have to make you, wicked witch, understand that I can't afford it? Please make this all stop. I was now getting very frustrated and furious, to say the least. Faby tried to calm me down and begged me to try and see eye to eye with his mother, promising me that after it was all over we would have a life together. Stupid me! This was one of the many moments in which I should have made a run for it and got my life back; instead, I listened to him as always. He was so convincing and seemed sincere, and he gave me hope that once living together, we would finally have a life.

I did my best to make him happy and agreed to go to Monza the next day and have a look at wedding dresses with the old witch. Why, oh why did I agree? She was, of course, fussing over everything, saying what she thought I should wear and quite honestly damned embarrassing in the shop. These dresses weren't for me, not at my age, for heaven's sake. Then it occurred to me, tight as she is, who is going to pay? I was certainly not going to pay out of my own pocket for a dress that I didn't like just to please her. So if I was going to have to look like a stupid meringue then at least she should have to pay. It was already a huge sacrifice for me being someone I wasn't trying to make someone who hated me happy. At the mention of money, she went all quiet and we left the shop! That's it, then. If she's not even going to offer my wedding dress, I'm going to dress how I want and as cheap as possible. This is all a farce, anyway. Once home and Faby saw the look on his mother's face, he stepped in to calm the situation and asked me to make a compromise, and that was to at least dress up for the ceremony in white. Mother had to see me in white; otherwise, she wouldn't let us live together. For heaven's sake, more blackmail and torture. Just who does this witch think she is and will there ever come a time when she minds her own business? We haven't even had one day together since the civil ceremony in England, and she is already behaving in this possessive, jealous way. What have I let myself in for?

My friend Lucinda, who was going to be my maid of honour of sorts, had a friend who was a dressmaker and said that if I got some material from the market, maybe we could botch something up to wear without going over the top in spending. Good idea I thought, and I'll get a simple white trouser suit made, no frills and no huge expenses. I may even be able to dye the suit afterwards and use it again. After all, what is the point of spending money to buy something that you can only wear for one day? What a waste! I finally got Faby's approval on me dressing in white, and even though not a traditional wedding dress he thought that he could handle his mother on this occasion. Incredible, things are improving!

We did have to go to and fro for the fittings, but in the end, a nice simple suit came out with a pretty jacket and some fancy buttons. Now, with a nice bouquet, I will almost look like a bride. Easier said than done. Of course, I couldn't just get on with my little part of organising. The nasty witch now wanted to choose the flowers, which, however, I had to pay for! This continual interference was never going to end. You must be joking. I can't even choose my own flowers? According to her, the flowers had to be white, as should the dress. Here we go again, as always, when she thinks she is not going to get her way. She starts her usual ranting about what SHE wants, and the theatricals take place yet again. You know what I did? I had been looking at flower shops and bouquets on offer already, and I went to a shop that offered nontraditional bouquets. I ordered the most beautiful, huge bouquet of lovely flowers with all the colours under the sun. Jokes apart, my bouquet was absolutely beautiful. I was so pleased with it, and of course, with a white trouser suit, it went perfectly and certainly better than a boring white bouquet on a boring white trouser suit. This bouquet made all the difference. Stuff you! Boy, was I pleased!

Before the wedding farce in Italy, Faby was very keen to take me down south to meet his relatives. His dad's sister still lived there and he had a load of cousins and a best friend there. I was very excited as I would see a different part of Italy which I had never seen before and the little town was only a few minutes from the sea so it would be a great holiday.

It was an eleven hour drive of mostly motorway from the North in Milan to the South in Puglia. Although it wasn't as far as Palermo in the deep south of Italy, it was still a long way to go, and the first time that I had encountered such a long journey.

He explained that he had lived his childhood summers there as it was his father's birthplace and every year, it was an event for his father to come back home. When his father was young, job opportunities were very rare unless you had land to cultivate, and so many Southerners transferred up north, leaving family and friends, to work in the Breda.

The Breda factories developed in the early 20th century over a vast area between Sesto San Giovanni and Milan. Locomotives and electromechanics, the railway industry, forges, metalworking and aeronautics, were the production sectors. During the 80's, the factories could boast a huge number of 20.000 employees. One of their famous productions was the carriages for the Milanese underground trains.

These factories gave a huge opportunity for the poorer people in the South to earn a wage and have a life.

The factories, as with shops and other trades, all shut down for the whole month of August. This would give all the southern families time to go back home to their loved ones. On August 1st, every year for many years, there would be a mass exodus. It really was quite something to see the town gradually emptying completely. The centre of Milan was bad enough, but the neighbouring town of Sesto San Giovanni where the Breda factories were, would empty by the end of the day and be like a ghost town.

The town also hosted another huge industry called the Falck, and again, most of the workers were Southerners who had come up north looking for work. This was one of the oldest companies in the steel industry, so with the Falck and the Breda industries shutting down for August, you can imagine just how many people left the town that summer.

The poor people remaining in the city would have to live for the whole month with everything closed. No bread shop, no chemist, very few doctors on call just for emergencies, etc. Only about a quarter of public transport was available as they too were entitled to their holiday. It was indescribable. I think you would have to experience something so weird to be able to believe it. There was a sense of depression and sadness. A complete emptiness and sense of no hope. It was a very strange feeling indeed.

Nowadays, the Breda factories and the Falck industry are no longer in use, and some of the huge areas left by these two giants have been used for a new university and some for commercial use. There is also a little more European mentality towards work. Companies and offices will program shifts, and workers will now take turns for their holidays so that the shop or the company can remain open. Although production still stops and many shops are on holiday, you can find at least one chemist on call and one bread shop in the area, and with the huge growth of big shopping malls as well, which are always open, the general public is now catered for, and the city is a little less lonely.

Faby's father would set off on the 1st of August as the most part of the town. They would fill their little Fiat up to the brim and set off late at night. The heat was unbearable during the summer, and the cars of that era had no air conditioning or comforts, so the only preferable way to travel for a lot of people was at night with all the car windows open. It would take them hours to get there as forty years ago, the roads were not as developed as they are today, and there would be this huge mass exodus of all the factory workers returning to their hometowns down south for the summer. Queues upon queues and lots of patience. Armed with bottles of water and sandwiches for the trip, they would slowly make their way home.

Once there, they would all kip down in the aunt's tiny little house in town, which was rather like a ruin. In their first years, there was a bucket for a toilet, certainly no shower, just a tap to make do to wash yourself. His aunt was born there and had never left the town in her life.

There was only one sleeping area, so when Faby took me, the aunt kindly gave us her space and put a camp bed down in the kitchen area for herself. It really was like camping, and I had never quite seen anything like it. For them, it was normal, and just the thought of being on holiday for a month was a huge delight despite the meagre circumstances. The land workers, as his aunt had been, were very poor so to even have her own house, no matter the size or the state, was a very big thing.

The area was beautiful. The town centre had its little market square, and there were lots of little shops and bars. I couldn't wait to have a walk around, and as Faby was always tired and either wanted to sleep or stay with his aunt and chat I wandered out. His aunt asked me what I was doing and told me I should wait for my boyfriend, but it was hot, and I needed to get out.

Everyone was dressed up to the nines and I got lots of strange looks. I kept checking to see if I had something out of place and couldn't understand why people were staring at me.

When I got back, I asked about this strange behaviour. For me, I was in Italy and that was that. Little did I know that the North and the South are considered two different countries.

I was told that for a woman to go out, she should either be in the company of other girlfriends or accompanied by her husband. What! The fact that I had a little walk in daylight and not in the middle of the night didn't make any difference. It was assumed that as I was alone, I was on the manhunt looking to pick up someone. Well, that's a new one!

I loved walking and certainly couldn't wait for my boyfriend to be in the mood for a walk so, having told me that it wasn't dangerous and that I would only ruin my reputation, I decided to have my walk whenever I wanted anyhow!

If he was that worried about my reputation, then he would just have to make the effort to accompany me. Otherwise, even though I didn't want to show disrespect, I would have to ignore the mentality of the area.

That was the first surprise.

We hadn't been at Aunties that long when an avalanche of people started popping in. It is a habit that people leave their doors open, particularly in the summer period, so friends, neighbours, family, whatever and whoever can drop in. Word travels fast, and everyone seemed to know that Aunty's favourite nephew was in town. Faby's brother evidently had a bad reputation here as no one had a good word for him. He was also known here as a lazy scrounger, and people just put up with him because his father was born there.

Anyhow, he wasn't there now, fortunately so we might hopefully get a bit of time at the sea for ourselves.

That was not going to happen! Cousins and acquaintances flooded in with all sorts of questions and invites to lunch and dinner. It was never-ending, and we were never going to have the time to be able to accept all the invites.

Faby had his priority persons list, and everyone else would have to make do with a quick visit and just a pop-in for a coffee thing.

During the years, his father, who was quite a handyman, had put in a weeny shower given the space available, and it was at least possible to wash decently. The house was tiny but very characteristic. The ceiling had parts which were very high shaped like a dome in a church, whereas others were very low. In fact, to have a shower, you had to bend down as the ceiling reached about one meter in height! It was all open space and no privacy except for the tiny bathroom where his father somehow managed to put a door on the area. There was a tiny little gas plate in the kitchen area where his aunt would put a huge saucepan on at lunchtime to cook her homemade pasta. She would be up early in the morning with all her equipment, and you would see her pounding her dough and shaping the orecchiette with her thumbs until all the shapes were even. The shape resembled little ears, and they were all perfect. It was a work of art and delicious. The typical dish in the little town and in Puglia in general was Orecchiette con cime di rapa. The cime di rapa is a little bit like broccoli, and with a little olive oil, produced in the same town, it was a real treat for our taste buds.

This was a poor man's dining from war times. Fresh vegetables from the land, semolina, flour and water for the pasta, and even during these terrible times they were able to eat a good meal.

Their other wonderful speciality, probably known all over the world by now, was the bruschetta.

We would pick up some potato bread from the local bakery, still warm, just out of the oven and add a couple of fresh hand picked tomatoes with a drizzle of local olive oil and voilà lunch is ready.

The difference in taste in getting local produce to what I would buy from the supermarket in Milan was astounding. The tomatoes were so sweet it was like eating a fruit. Everything actually had a taste to it, and if you added a little local cheese, it would be a dinner fit for a king, which I would pay pounds for very willingly.

Faby had many relatives who were farmers or olive growers, and one day, we went visiting and actually took part in making the local cheese with them. His cousin was a typical happy, smiling, overweight lady who was sitting on a three-legged wooden stool. The stool was at least five times smaller than she was, and she sat in front of a huge wooden barrel with her very large apron on. It was such a typical image and very funny in a nice way. She was stirring the curdling milk with a huge wooden spoon. This would eventually become a delicious "cacioricotta" cheese. Some were already in their containers, which are called "fruscelle." They are like tiny baskets but made from plastic and the small holes allow the liquid to filter to the bottom and the cheese to remain soft but not drowning in liquid. She offered us one just made and still warm. It's such a Moorish treat, and you just can't stop eating once you start. It goes down so well, and with a drop of wine, I could have carried on for the whole day!

I didn't want to leave but we had so many visits to make we had to be on our way.

The next stop was a brother and sister who were now pensioners. They had worked on the land their entire lives growing olive trees and picking the olives when ready, which would then be used to produce local olive oil. Their little house in the vast expanse of olive trees was still being habited, but as they had worked all their lives and had saved hard they were in the process of moving to town to a "proper" house.

They were so sweet. They were like a couple, really, and if you didn't know it, you wouldn't realise that they were, in fact, brother and sister.

They were so fond of each other, such a humble couple it was quite overwhelming. Again, as other members of the family we were meeting, they also had never ever been out of the area in their whole lives and certainly weren't worldly, but they had such a kind pureness about them and an obvious love for the countryside and their work that I found it quite emotional. Nothing like the big-headed jacket and tie types that I have to put up with every day in Milan, but just something so simple and genuine. It really was a breath of fresh air.

I loved these people with their genuine personalities right from the start.

I felt like I was living in a time gone by, and I think that it was probably the only time I was really truly happy with my husband-to-be.

The brother and sister were very proud of their achievement in saving up and buying a house, and so, of course, we got an invite for the next day.

They had managed to buy a beautiful big villa just on the outskirts of town with a huge rooftop terrace.

Another thing I learnt during this period was that when someone wanted you to feel welcome they would offer you a tour of their home. It was their way of letting you into their lives and making you feel a part of them. This had never happened to me in England and was a bit strange at first, but the more people we visited, the more house tours I received, and I got to enjoy them very much.

It's a big part of their hospitality traditions and in fact, did make me feel very welcome indeed.

The rather oversized sister, with her big apron, opened the door to us and invited us in.

The ground floor was a huge garage, very typical of the houses in the area. The rather humorous situation to me was that this garage was also used as a living area, again very typical of the area.

The car was parked in the garage on one side, where there was also a small bathroom, something like a workshop bathroom, that you would find in a mechanic's garage.

On the other side of this huge space was a kitchen. It was the sort of kitchen you would find somewhere like Ikea, very everyday and practical. Then, in the middle was a large table, some chairs and a big armchair for the brother.

We were invited to sit down and offered some homemade limoncello which was served from old vinegar jars. This is where they lived and ate and only used the upstairs accommodation to sleep.

After a bit of chit-chat, we were then shown around. The sister opened a big door at the back of the garage, which was the entrance to the "proper" house. We immediately found ourselves in front of a very large staircase which would take us upstairs. The stairs were immensely wide and made of beautiful, shiny Italian marble with a decorated wrought iron handrail. I was absolutely astounded. It was so beautiful and, quite honestly, a work of art in itself.

We were shown upstairs, where there must have been at least 400 square meters of living accommodation. We were shown the two big bedrooms, which were the only rooms they used upstairs, a beautiful luxury kitchen and bathroom again with luxury marble everywhere, and a really enormous living room with luxury furniture.

Everything was perfect, having never been used. It looked like a show house and they were quite rightly very proud. However, the garage was their living space, and that's how it was!

The sister then opened another door, which took us to another level where we found an enormous terrace giving a view over the whole town and the sea. It was breathtaking. They had fitted the terrace out with tables, big sunshades and a huge barbecue.

I was very pleased with this pleasant couple. After a lifetime of work to achieve something like this, it was very heartwarming.

It just goes to show that one should never ever judge appearances. This elderly couple, after so many years of living in the middle of acres of olive trees with not a human being in sight, and having never left the village, had bought the most wonderful villa and furnished it impeccably.

The fact that they don't actually use this beautiful house but prefer to live in the garage, eating at a table with a view of their old banger of a car, well, that's a different matter!!

CHAPTER 14

Hospitality is a little overwhelming at times, and what always used to make me laugh was the same question we used to get asked by everyone. As soon as we arrived, word got around, and all and sundry would pop in and give out their invites for lunch or dinner. They would immediately ask how long we were staying and when we were going back. Heavens, we have only just arrived, and you are already asking me when I'm leaving! It was the same story from everyone each time. The first couple of years, I went along with accepting the invites, but it was all a bit too much as it didn't leave any time to go to the sea or just have a bit of a holiday, just public relations from morning till night. As if this wasn't enough, most of the people who invited us wanted to see us again, and even when explaining that there was a whole list of people to see and the time was limited, they would be offended if we didn't go round again.

It's all very nice, but there is a limit. Of course, if I said anything, my opinion was worthless, and all this visiting had to be done. It was exhausting. The following year, he obliged his best friend Big M "Sponge" to come with us.

Sponge was a childhood friend from the Sesto area where Faby and his family lived and did not have a happy family environment. As a consequence, he was always with us like an adopted child. He also exaggerated his love for super alcoholic drinks, hence his nickname Sponge. Not only did he drink me out of the house and home, but never once did he think to bring a bottle himself or offer us a pizza. He used to cost me a fortune, but as he was Faby's best friend all was granted. When we finally had permission from the wicked witch to live together, it got to the point where I would automatically set the table for three knowing that he would turn up and there was nothing I could do about it.

It was already a miracle that the first year we went down South alone, as in the years to come, I realised that this would never happen again and that if his family or friends were not tagging along, there was no way we would do anything as a couple. Nevertheless, Sponge being present made things a little easier on me, all things considered, as no one there were relatives of his and he wasn't having his holiday spoilt by PR work all day. Faby had to start inventing things for his friend Sponges' benefit and tried to be diplomatic in refusing some invites. This, however, only came about because his friend told him that he was totally exaggerating in being Mr nice guy and trying to do right by everyone except me. I had been telling him the same thing, but my opinion didn't count. Anyhow, in the end, it's the result that counts, and thankfully, we did have a bit more time to go to the sea as a threesome! Better than nothing.

It was a relief for me as, from the very first visit, I hadn't been accepted at all by his aunt. She would deliberately speak in dialect in front of me but with her back turned to make me feel invisible. I love the different dialects, always listen attentively, and have actually been able to pick up a few words. In any case, I got the gist of what she was saying, which wasn't very pleasant. She told Faby that she was very disappointed with his choice of marrying a foreigner. She had someone in mind from the town who he should be marrying, and he knew this jolly well. This decision wasn't acceptable to her! She was very offensive with her words and kept referring to me as "quella lì" (that over there), refusing to use my name and treating me as an object.

I'd already been through the threats of his mother about wanting to kill me if I took her son away, and now this. Well, we are in for a good time, aren't we?

I told him to have a talk with her and explain that this was his choice and not hers and that she should respect his choice if she wanted to keep up a good relationship with him.

Strangely enough, for the first and only time in his life, he was a man about it and told her very nicely exactly that. From that moment, she did her best to be civil to me, and during the years to come, we actually got on a lot better than I did with his mother.

I wish he had followed my advice with his mother as we wouldn't be in the terrible situation we are today if only he had had the guts to put her in her place as well. Unfortunately, that was not to be and the outcome would be disastrous.

Our first visit together in Puglia was also to introduce me to his other best friend, who would also be his best man at the wedding, so I was looking forward to meeting him.

Ennio was a really nice, friendly guy who worked as a carpenter with his father for the family business. We went to see them at their workplace, where both Ennio and his father were present, and they made me very welcome. We got on immediately, and I willingly accepted their invitation to meet the rest of the family.

It was a large family with three other sisters, a mother and a grandmother. As it was summer, they had left their townhouse to go to the Selva, an area just above the town and a little bit cooler away from the town centre heat. Most of the locals would do this in the summer, and although this area was only a few minute's drive from the town, it actually was a lot cooler, and a lot of the town's habitants transferred to their holiday homes big or small to get away from the noise and the heat. It seemed strange having a holiday home only a few minutes from town, but the area was beautiful, and for the working people, it was ideal as they could get away from the hustle and bustle but still be near to work and at the same time feel on holiday.

Ennio's family had a lovely villa with lots of ground in the midst of olive trees and countryside, and was wonderfully peaceful. They used the terrace and grounds to have barbecues and eat outside.

They all made me so welcome and, from day one, treated me as if I were part of the family. It was such a nice feeling to not be judged or threatened for once. The grandmother was a real card, and although she only spoke dialect, she took a liking to me, and in some way, we managed to communicate. She was such a laugh, and it was as if I had known them forever. The mother's cooking was spectacular, and I got to taste all the local dishes they prepared. They were down to earth people with big hearts and big hospitality. The portions were so big that I could never manage to finish my plate, and it took me weeks to get them to give me a smaller portion without them feeling offended that I didn't like the food. Only eventually, having smaller portions just for me, was I able to finish the delicious grilled fish or the orecchiette pasta that was served. Wherever I went, it was always the same phrases, finish up your food or I will be offended! I did like the food, but boy, was it difficult to make them understand that it was way too much. Sometimes, the mother would just keep piling things on my plate as a sign of hospitality, or she would offer me more parmesan cheese for my pasta, which she would serve, literally taking a handful and sprinkling it on the pasta. It was so funny. They really were my adopted family for many years after that.

Because of the heat, their lunch break would become a siesta and work would commence about four o'clock in the afternoon in summer, which meant finishing work would be around 9 pm. We would have to wait for Ennio's work to finish to go out in the evenings to eat together, and so sometimes we didn't start eating till about 10 pm. This was very normal here, and the restaurants were open till late. I had to get used to these strange hours, but it was pleasant eating outside in the cool in the midst of olive trees after the heat of the day.

While we were there, Ennio suggested places to visit, and we did manage to escape from our PR duties and went off to Alberbello which was the highlight for me. This is a city of drystone dwellings known as "trulli." It was a fairytale dream.

These buildings were constructed using roughly worked limestone boulders collected from neighbouring fields and, later, the large water-collecting basins in the area. They are a remarkable example of prehistorical building techniques. I can understand why they are on the World Heritage list and would strongly recommend visiting this fairytale place.

It was such a unique little town, I had never seen anything like it, and with these small round white houses with their dome-shaped grey rooftops it really made me feel as though I was stepping back in time.

Of course, you cannot take a trip to the south of Italy without seeing at least a few of their many traditional religious festivities and as it was August the town of Locorotondo nearby would be having its' protector saint St Rocco festival.

This important festival begins with a big village fair and continues for three days. The town is decorated with blazing lights, and on the last day, Saints Day, there is a dirge played along the town's streets, liturgical ceremonies and a corteo of costumes and colours. Although it was interesting, I found it all a bit heavy going in the end and much preferred the lighter atmosphere of the marketplace in the town where Auntie lived. Here, it was just simply a celebration of summer life. Everyone was out on the streets and in the marketplace to take advantage of the cooler evening temperatures after the terrible heat of the day. All the shops are open until very late, and the butcher's shops put stands out lining the streets right outside their shops. They cook their meats to order so you can have a snack while standing on your feet and watching the world go by. They have a wood-burning oven and will cook and grill right from the butcher's. Trying out their lamb or sausage specialities was quite a delight and certainly a different way of eating out in the evening, I loved it.

I also loved my walks in the market square and around the town. I took no notice of the stares and just got on with my trip out. Ennio's family was wonderful, and all in all, I had a lovely time. After the chat with his Aunt, things were a little less strained, and so, as for my first visit to Puglia is concerned, I can really say that it was a success.

CHAPTER 15

The big day of the Italian wedding finally came, and for me it was a poor turnout in that only my family came. I couldn't afford to pay for my friends as tradition would have it, and my London friend at the time decided for some reason not to come. So, in the end, I just had my small group to pay for and my own choice of Bomboniere presents for my small group of invites. My two bridesmaids were Italian, and one of them came all the way from America and interrupted her holiday just to be there, and that was hugely appreciated, given my small turnout.

The church was full of his side of the family, and it was a short but sweet service by a couple of pleasant priests who didn't hesitate to invite themselves for a freebie lunch at the lake after the service! What can you do? That's how things go over here!

After the service, we all got into our cars and made off for the lakes, going through Como and into a tiny little village with a restaurant on the waterfront. A very beautiful setting and good for some pictures. I refused to have pictures done at the church in the middle of the city with all its grey and smog. The weather was beautiful, and the restaurant had good service and food, so all was well. When it came to the photos, the wicked witch just couldn't contain herself any longer and had to become the centre of attention, once again conveniently forgetting that the Bride should have her day. She started bossing people about to have photos taken with her. Nobody was interested, of course, but to keep her quiet, most people gave in, and she got her way as usual.

She had come up to the North from a small town outside of Napoli many years ago, had had no schooling and couldn't really speak Italian, being used to speaking in dialect. You can just imagine the laughs we had when she tried to speak to my family. Brits who couldn't speak a word of Italian and a Neapolitan who could speak either Italian or English! Why is it that when people who don't speak the same language think it is enough to raise their voice and gesticulate, miraculously, the other person will understand what you are saying? It was so embarrassing but, at the same time, hugely funny, and we all had a good laugh at her expense. My father, who is a very patient man, did his best to humour her, and she couldn't stop talking about how wonderful he was for the next few weeks.

We spent the evening with friends and family and stayed by the lakes till the next day. Then, off to the Amalfi coast for a week.

As it was the month of May, the weather was beautiful, and it was not tourist season yet, so very quiet. It was such a beautiful area, and I can still remember their special lemon profiteroles which I have never seen or eaten anywhere else in Italy. As it was low season, we were given an upgrade, which was a pretty ordinary hotel. By giving us an upgrade and the use of their one and only suite with a huge balcony, it was a dream. Of course, Fabrizio had to call mother three times a day, even on our honeymoon, which was a bit of a pain. Being reminded of her constantly on my honeymoon was not what I would call healthy, but all in all, it was a very pleasant stay and probably one of the very few nice moments together looking back. At least on this occasion, he had no excuses whatsoever to bring his friends along!

We had some nice trips out and the characteristic restaurants were beautiful. A lot were on the seafront and one in particular had been excavated in the sea rocks. Although it was terribly humid inside, of course, it was still a great experience.

There were a lot of stalls in the small alleyways, and most of them sold porcelain objects. They were all handmade and typical of the area. The colours were beautiful, and I couldn't resist buying a couple of pots as a souvenir.

CHAPTER 16

So back to work and finally living in the same flat together. After all, we have been officially married for some time now, and mother had got her way regarding a church service, so now there were no excuses on earth that she could possibly find to keep her son under the same roof as her and she was not at all pleased!

I had waited nearly a year after our marriage to have permission to live with my own husband. It better have been worth the wait!

It was a pity that instead of beginning a new life together, the nightmare was just about to begin.

I would get home from work, and my mother would call. In those days, mobile phones still had not been invented, and so she would call on the landline and want to speak to me. She would interrogate me as to what I had cleaned and in what condition I had left the house in the morning and told me to get rid of my duvet as her son was used to sleeping with a sheet and blanket. Do I have any choice here? I thought. Her main hobby, however, was food. She would call every evening to ask what I was cooking. Nothing was ever right. This or that was not acceptable and if for once I was making something that in her opinion was worthy of her wonderful son she would be on the phone for ages telling me exactly in what way it should be cooked and for how long because he would only eat it in a certain way. It was driving me crazy, and I asked him to have a word with her and tell her to stop interfering. Of course, that did not happen, as it would have been a lack of respect towards his mother, according to him. But what about the lack of respect towards me? No, on the contrary, mother comes first, and her word is sacred. She must be obeyed! My goodness, she would have been such a good Gestapo boss.

At the weekends she would insist on her son going to pick her up so that she could come shopping with us. Every Saturday morning he would have to get up early and couldn't sleep in on his day off. She said she had to teach me how and what to shop for, what pieces of meat to ask for and ingredients to buy for her son. I was already over 30 and had been living on my own for years. If I wasn't capable of doing my own shopping by now, there was something wrong, don't you think? I certainly didn't need madam interfering and telling me how to do things.

On one of these many occasions, we were in the butcher's shop for so long that I could have brought a camp bed and had a kip! She was bartering away with the butcher so fiercely that I walked out, totally embarrassed. We were doing the shopping for us with my wage, and all she could do was boss us about and even tell me how to spend my wage on food shopping. Incredible, I can't stand this much more. Of course, when she came out of the butcher's, I got such a bollocking from her as if I was the one who had been rude. My wonderful husband just stood there hanging his head as usual. This is a good start, I thought. I wonder what else is to come.

Not only was I under scrutiny for how I cleaned and how I cooked but she also insisted that we spend every Sunday with her as well as she couldn't bear the thought of not seeing her son every day. Not content with him there every lunch time during the working week from Monday to Friday, we were also expected to sacrifice our weekends for her and not just once in a while but every awful Sunday! This went on for a while, and then I just exploded and demanded that my husband spend a weekend with me for once. After all, we talked about one day in the week for me, given that he spent the other six days with that witch. I managed to convince him, and we went out for the day to the lakes and had a nice, pleasant walk and a coffee out together. Things that should be jolly normal and not to be fought for in my opinion.

The next Sunday guess where we had to go? To see mummy, of course! It was as though years had gone by and not just one weekend. Off she went with her theatrical ranting and raving. Bollocking after bollocking, bawling about how insensitive and selfish I was taking her son away from her and, how dare I expect him to have time with me, his wife when his duty was to be with her! Here we go again. There really is a limit to my patience, and I can see it very quickly coming to an end.

This time, I retaliated. To try and be correct, I first had a quick word with my husband, but there was no reasoning with him. He was completely under her thumb and scared stiff. That was it; a huge row took place, and we took our leave.

I felt so sorry for his father who just sat there helpless. His father was a lovely man and always nice to me. You would never ever hear him say a bad word about anyone, and he liked us going to visit. He, unlike his awful wife, however, would never oblige us to go and was just pleased to see us when we did find time. He could do nothing to stop his wife from bawling her lungs out at me, and given the expression on his face, I saw he was unfortunately used to it and had given up trying many years ago.

Of course, according to the witch, I was in the wrong and according to my husband, too! I mean, after all, I was only his wife and had no rights whatsoever!

I tried to explain to him that she must learn to leave us alone, and he must stop spoiling her and doing everything that she orders him to do. We have a right to our own lives. This does not mean that he should never see her again but he must make an effort to spend a little less time with mummy and more as a couple. He seemed to understand, but as the weeks went by, there was no improvement whatsoever. The only person who defended me a little was his father. He was certainly more understanding than his wife. He was also fed up with her bossiness and had always said that he would have been happier in a real prison rather than the prison he was actually in. She was hated in the whole neighbourhood, had no friends, and even her nephews hated her for her frustrating way of poking her nose into anything that didn't concern her. Unfortunately, I was officially married, and evidently, I had married the family and not my husband, but I was still not ready to give up.

CHAPTER 17

We started life in my tiny 30 square meter "monolocale" studio flat. You couldn't swing a cat in it, let alone have parties. Nonetheless, I seemed to find myself cooking every evening for his friends and trying to squash in people while doing the cooking, serving and washing up. It just wasn't on the cards to have some alone time, and he did not really accept the few people I knew, so it was always his friends who were there and, quite honestly, not my cup of tea.

There was big M Sponge, who was a very frequent visitor. He was another one who, like the family, accused me of taking away his best friend and ruining his life. He had family problems with a harsh father and, as mentioned earlier, came nearly every night to escape from home life. His favourite pastime was getting through a bottle of Jägermeister from the moment he arrived to when he left, which was always extremely late. When you are just getting through the month and trying to make ends meet, at the beginning all these extra expenses become very heavy going. Not only would he take advantage and never do anything in exchange but he was always needing some sort of favour. Never could my husband find the courage to say no or put him off for one evening now and again and say that we would see him another night as he was spending time with me. Sponge had precedence over me, just like mother and the rest of the family, and many rows were the consequence.

As if this wasn't enough, I used to find other friends of his ringing the bell in the evening, expecting to eat and drink. One couple were actually quite nice but very possessive and not at all sensitive. They used to invite themselves without warning and would stay until one in the morning when I had to get up early for work the next day. Of course, Faby would not say a word and enjoyed having them there all evening rather than having to spend time alone with me. At first, it was fun, and I was having a social life which I hadn't had in England, but as time went on, it really was too much. I was the one who had to stand up and basically throw them out when it got late. When I tried to say now and again that we had something else to do for an evening and we would see them another time, they would be terribly offended and ask exactly where we were going, who with and why. And as if that wasn't enough, they would ask to come too! There just didn't seem to be a way around it. When were we going to have a bit of a life, just the two of us?

Added to this there was also the problem of family events. Every Easter, birthday or Christmas, we were expected to go to his brother's for lunch or dinner, and that also became a nightmare and the origin of many, many fights. There was no choice. That is how it's done here, I would be told, and as I was the guest in a foreign country, I was expected to fit in and live according to their traditions, which I did try in the beginning.

When October came around, the wicked witch started her ranting and raving about Christmas three months in advance. She would either call and go on for hours or make a scene when we popped around. Her favourite phrase to her son, and obviously in front of me for my benefit, was that this could be her last Christmas as she was getting on a bit and in no way should he consider going away with me for that period as she needed her son by her side. The Neapolitan theatricals kicked in as usual, and there were crocodile tears and gesticulations of all sorts and her begging with all her heart that her son should not abandon such a poor elderly person in such a time that was meant for the family, which is so sacred! This has been going on for 25 years, and the old bat is still alive and kicking and, as they say in Italian, literally translated, "rompendo le palle," breaking our balls!

I tried to do my best during the first few years and went very unwillingly to these events. His sister-in-law would have all of her family around, plus Faby's mother and father, and I really didn't feel that I fit in. I was a "pesce fuor d'acqua," I felt like a fish out of water and not accepted in any way. However, small people's flats seem to be of no interest to the family. All that matters is that the whole family is there, whether squashed like sardines, as in this case or not. They can even hate each other during the year and not speak, but at Christmas, you have to play happy families and pretend that everything is wonderful, like the films you see on TV.

It was such a farce. I had never seen anything like it.

Of course, this meant a big stage as far as my mother-in-law was concerned and just could not be left unused. As soon as all were present in the rabbit hutch, it was as though someone had pressed a start button and off she went. The moaning and groaning would commence. The complaints about everything and everyone, and all present, out of respect, would remain in silence while she had her say. It was like a broken record. I must have heard her stories about a million times, always the same and always to and about the same people. Obviously, having no friends, this was her only occasion of having a big audience and being the centre of attention and having no other arguments or hobbies to speak about we would be bored for hours listening to her rantings.

After a couple of years of this farce, I would get up from the table and go out on the balcony as a sign of personal protest. Of course very disrespectful from their point of view but enough is enough. The other thing that really got my back up about these lunches was Faby's brother. This guy reminded me of a big toad, which is probably offensive to a toad. He was a lazy lard! He would just manage to get a "hello" out of his mouth to greet people as they came in and then would take his place at the head of the table. From that moment on, he would neither move nor speak but expect to be waited on and revered. I sometimes thought that we were living in a different century seeing him there with his unfriendly, rude behaviour.

For instance, even when a bottle of water, wine or whatever was right in front of him, he would order his wife or his daughter to get up from the other end of the table and pour what he wanted into his glass! Never once did he get up to take a dirty dish to the kitchen, and heaven forbid the thought of him washing something! Once he had taken his place at the head of the table there, he would stay throughout the hours of boredom and wouldn't even get up to say goodbye when people started leaving, and the get-together was at an end. This guy just did his job in the week, didn't bother to get on in life and once home, remained seated waiting for the women to do everything. He had no interests, and although his wage was rather a minimum one, he couldn't be bothered to do further education to get a better job possibility. Years later, I discovered that my husband was giving his wage to the lazy scrounging lout, so what did he care about making an effort? Quite honestly, I wouldn't have given him the time of day if I hadn't been forced to.

Another one who had a built-in start button without a switch off was the guy's wife, Faby's sister-in-law, and as I found out in years to come, the commander of the whole family. Appearances can be deceiving, and although the husband seemed to be in command with his strange behaviour in the home, it was, in fact, completely the opposite.

Once the wicked witch had finished her horrendously boring speech with her usual complaining, that was the cue for freedom of speech for anyone else at the table. However, easier said than done. Instead of the lunch becoming somewhat more normal and the possibility of having a reasonable conversation with someone resembling at least slightly interesting or intelligent, that would all be put on hold. The sister-in-law's push-button would suddenly flare up, figuratively speaking and off she would go. You could see her eyes light up with the suspense of waiting for her turn to have the stage free and the moment had now finally arrived. It was rather like a sort of revenge on her mother-in-law now she was going to take the attention away from her and that was a great sense of power and quite delightful for her.

Off she would go, complaining about what a bad week it had been. What a migraine with all those bad children she taught at school, and what a difficult life she had. She was the only teacher of infants who worked so hard, the only one on the face of the earth who suffered from migraines and the only one who had to do so much. This was yet again another of the broken record situations which we have heard continuously for a quarter of a century! So another hour went by, listening to the "lady" of the house trying to show an interested expression without yawning.

Once coffee had been served, quite honestly, I couldn't wait to leave, but no, that would be, of course, too simple, wouldn't it? I then had the problem of convincing my husband very discreetly to leave, and asap!! As Faby was the brother, he felt he had to be the last to leave out of politeness, and of course, appearances are what matter here. So even if he was as bored as I was he would show me one of those facial expressions of his which said everything. There was nothing I could do. After a few years of this I just couldn't take it anymore and said that I had decided not to participate in these family meetings. That did not go down well at all, as you can imagine. I heard everything from what people think to how they will be offended and a hundred other excuses, which, by this time, I couldn't give a toss!

CHAPTER 18

During this time, I had started my new office job, which I really liked. I had a Portuguese lady boss who was really cool, and we got on well. The office was in San Babila in the centre of Milan and just a couple of minutes from Via della Spiga, where all the top designer fashion was to be found. It made for a nice walk on my lunch break and, of course, only window shopping for me as you can imagine the prices. I was very surprised at the lack of care for the city, particularly in the centre. There was a small park just off Corso Venezia, but you had to be careful where you walked as it was full of syringes and obviously a meeting place for druggies.

What a shame and what a waste of taxpayer's money! So that was crossed off my list of lunch break walks, and I kept to the centre pavements. La Scala theatre was also nearby, and the shopping mall was near to the cathedral. This four-story double arcade in central Milan was quite interesting to see. It's called Galleria Vittorio Emanuele II and connects the cathedral square, Piazza del Duomo. If you walk out in the other direction, you come out at Piazza della Scala where the big theatre is. There is an octagonal space in the centre of the mall, which is topped with a glass dome and it was under this space that I would see a lot of tourists right in the middle turning around. It was very curious and quite funny to see all these tourists doing such strange things, so I had to find out what they were doing. The ground was very pretty, with four mosaics, one of which was Turin's coat of arms. This consisted of a bull, and the tradition was, as I found out, that if a person spins around three times with a heel on the bull's testicles, poor thing, this will bring him good luck. In fact, it is such a tradition that a hole has now developed in the place of the poor bull's genitals!

I continued learning with my new job and worked my way up to personal assistant and budget manager for the office. It was too good to be true, of course, as always! A new girl was hired to help out with the secretarial work, and as there were only four of us in the office and lots of work, it would be a welcome help. She came from a humble background and was very intelligent and a quick learner. In fact too quick! Seeing how life is in Milan and being surrounded by very rich people, she just couldn't keep her feet on the ground, nor her hands off a rich married colleague! And so her campaign to better herself at other people's expense commenced. My other female colleague could also see what was happening, but nobody was going to stop her. She broke up our male colleagues' marriage in the end and so desperately wanted to be a part of the higher class life that she would stop at nothing. He came from a different background to myself and my other colleague, having lawyer parents and being rather high up in society etc. It was such a temptation for this kid to creep up the social ladder that she just couldn't resist. She created many problems in the office, and just when our boss decided to do something about it, as she was making everyone's life hell, another bombshell exploded.

Our boss was a very nice lady and got paid a considerably high wage that was quite incredible even by Milan standards. She had her luxury flat paid for, various expenses, and travel all as part of her wage, so I really couldn't complain. Unfortunately, she would use her office expense card for personal use as well, which obviously shouldn't have been done. She certainly didn't need a bigger wage to buy clothes or other personal purchases, and even if she bought designer clothes and ate out at the best restaurants with her own money, there would still be a huge amount left at the end of the month. However, temptation got the better of her and the situation was evidently too much to handle. It seems the more you have, the more you want.

Head office started asking questions about her expenses, and I found myself caught between wanting to be loyal to my boss and not wanting to lie. This problem, however, was resolved, for me at least, in that my female colleague decided she wanted a bit of fame and a pat on the back and decided to take matters into her own hands. She called head office and told them what was going on. Before we knew it we had a visit from one of the big bosses and were told to gather in the meeting room. He said that our lady boss had been suspended. In fact, she hadn't shown up for work that day and that the matter would be handled internally.

To avoid explanations to the tax office or any other explanations in general, they were shutting the office down, and we were all sacked! I nearly fainted and couldn't believe what my colleague had done. This should have been handled with discretion, but her wish to be somebody important for five minutes and get credit from head office had not only backfired on her, but we were now all without a job. Big boss stood up, showed us the door and there was no room for discussion. All out. Great!

Our male colleague of course, would have no problem in finding another job with his circle of friends and acquaintances and his new girlfriend would go and live with him. That left my other traitor colleague and good riddance to her and me. So, back to square one and on the hunt again for a new job.

CHAPTER 19

Fortunately, I was still at an age where it was just possible for a woman to still be accepted for work and not considered too old, so I managed to find something and start from the beginning again. Of course, it was a minimum wage and back to the grindstone, but I had no choice and started off as a receptionist for an international consulting firm, again in the centre of Milan. The job consisted of very long hours, but one or two of my colleagues were quite nice, and I also found another English girl who was working as a secretary, so I settled in quite well. The company was very rich and successful. Business was going well, which meant they had money to spend on frivolities so there were lots of after-work parties which I had to attend. I didn't really like that as it meant getting home really late, but it was considered rude not to attend and, above all, part of the job.

During this time and having found a new job, I could finally look for a new apartment with a little bit more space. The prices were too high in the city which meant looking in the country area a few kilometres away. I found a nice little two-bedroomed flat with a country train station a couple of kilometres by foot away so I could get into work.

You will find absolutely nothing furnished over here, which means your purchase is just the four walls and you have to then budget carefully for the extras like a kitchen and furniture. I had nothing from my old flat except a bed, so everything would have to be bought from scratch.

I managed to get a mortgage on my wage and went ahead. The flat, however, was still inhabited, and the people said that they were also looking to buy a house but hadn't yet found one. They had put the house on the market, and the purchase could go ahead, but the new owners, i.e. myself, would have to wait for the keys until the vendor had found a new house. This was all very well but I wanted a deadline in any case as

I couldn't wait for them to take all the time in the world if I was going to fork out the money but have to wait for the keys to the house.

We came to an agreement on the date on which they must leave, whether they find a new house or not, which seemed to be ample time for both parties.

I put my little flat up for sale, and it sold pretty quickly, but the owners of my future flat, even when the deadline arrived, refused to leave. I tried to put pressure on the estate agency, who should have insisted that they leave as that was their job, and the contract should be made to be respected.

Unfortunately, we are talking about Italy, where nothing seems to work out, and I couldn't physically throw them out! They evidently had no conscience about respecting the deadline; the estate agency couldn't care less, and there was nothing I could do.

At this point, I suggested to my husband that we get a cheap motel in the meantime just to get through these few weeks, but guess what he wanted to do? Yes, he wanted to go back to mummy! There was no reasoning with him; as usual, he could be very persuasive, putting it on an economic level and how much we could save by staying with his parents. They also had a tiny one-bedroom flat, and I didn't like the idea at all. I had no choice, as usual, and we kipped down there. It was a disaster. She had her son under her roof now, and the interference was horrendous.

Being under the same roof, she could not only interfere but also keep control over everything. She could see what time we got home from work, what to eat, whether we went out or not. I suggested that we should at least go out every evening as it was bad enough living with them, but to spend all our free time too like this was just not acceptable to me. His mother put her foot down saying that we were not to spend by going out as we were buying a house. I told her that it was none of her business, but my husband stood up for her and told me to shut up as I was being disrespectful to her in her house. He said we must not offend her and, therefore, we should pass every evening after work cooped up listening to her complaints. He wouldn't budge from his point of view, and we didn't have the possibility of even having a private conversation as she would not allow it. It was hell, and I was losing my mind. Living on top of each other in a prison cell was not for me. I was considering moving out myself into a motel and leaving him with his mother just to get through the time necessary, but he kept hammering me, telling me how selfish I was and what his mother would think etc, etc. He made me feel really awful and as though my suggestions were something alien.

As if this wasn't enough, I also had to put up with his niece. His sister-in-law worked and had no time for her daughter. She was also very tight and preferred leaving the kid with the nasty old witch rather than paying a babysitter. I wonder how this kid is going to grow up, I used to think. That made for five of us living in forty square meters. The little girl was very attached to my husband in an uncanny way. It made the hairs stand up on my skin, but I couldn't really find a reason, and in the end, I thought that she was just a kid and would grow out of it. It was a very strange sensation, and she got all of the attention. I thought that perhaps I was making a mountain out of a molehill, but this nagging sensation never left me over the years; instead of growing out of it, the situation got worse. In fact, this little kid was going to be my downfall and would go on to do dastardly things!

CHAPTER 20

Thankfully, the couple who were in our new house to be finally found a place of their own, and we could get on with furnishing and moving in. It was tough on a basic wage so I had to do things little by little when I could, but I got the kitchen installed and had a bed, so that is how we started. We used wooden fruit boxes to sit on, but at least I was in my own place and not living with his awful mother. Anything was better than that! Faby was a labourer, so his wage was even less than mine, but it still should have been a help and better than only one wage. However, we seemed to have huge difficulties getting through to the end of the month. I found out later that he was giving his wage to his family, no wonder it was always difficult.

Now we had a bigger flat and a nice balcony, there was even more room for his friends and I would find my house completely full when I got home from work and was expected to cook sometimes for as many as a dozen people. The flat was in a nice quiet area and although it meant me getting up at dawn to get the train and then the underground to get into Milan I was pleased with my choice. When I got home from work, it was like being on holiday as I was out of the noise of the city and the first few years were very pleasant. The only exception, of course, was that I rarely could enjoy this peace because the house would be full of people.

The condominium was a three-storey building with a total of nine families, so a very small environment compared to other areas. This is one of the reasons I chose it, hoping for some peace and quiet. In all these situations, there is always a bad apple, and whether you are in a three-family environment or a thirty-family situation, there will always be somebody to spoil your life. In this condominium, there was a family on the second floor who were very nosey. Right at the beginning, the guy came knocking on the door to introduce himself. He started off with all his questions of what do you do, how much do you earn and really personal questions. I don't like to be rude, but as the weeks went by and nearly every night, he would come by not only to ask questions but to try and scrounge something, I had to learn to be a bit tougher and say I was in the middle of something and not invite him in. I wasn't educated like that, and it was hard at first but if I didn't, he basically would have moved in!

Then there was the couple on the same floor as us. They were older than us, and the wife was a manager in a hospital and very proud of it. The problem was she liked to make a point of letting all and sundry know just how important she was; consequently, the rest of us were really little nobodies. Faby loves that type of person, and with his charm and foxiness, she soon took a shine to him, and they got very friendly. Her husband then started calling in as soon as he got home from work. In the beginning, that was ok, and I would offer him a glass of wine, but as his wife was so important and would work late, he would take advantage of us being home earlier to stay with us. I would wait and wait before cooking our meal, and it got later and later. In the end, I used to set the table for three as it was the only way to eat at a decent time. He had no sensitivity at all for others, and many evenings, he would be there till midnight without a care in the world.

Again, in the beginning, I would stay up while he was conversing with Faby. I told him that he must be a bit firmer and stop letting all and sundry into my house and that I had a right to some free evenings without being surrounded by others constantly. Of course, he wouldn't listen and do nothing, so it got to the stage where, about ten or eleven, I would say I was tired, and I would go off to bed and read. According to the way I was brought up, it would be considered rude, but when you get to your limit of patience you have to change your outlook on things. This went on for months, and because Faby had had enough, too, he used to go to the bar after work and come home late to avoid the neighbours. I would have to put up with him for an hour or two until he finally realised that my husband would be late, and with me, there was no conversation to be had and left.

This way of life went on for a few years. It was tolerable as long as I had my peace and quiet but that too was about to end.

CHAPTER 21

On the second floor underneath my flat was a young couple who had an eight-year-old daughter. The father was a flower power ex-hippie and still lived in those times. The wife was a strong character control freak and the husband had to do as he was told. He idolised his daughter, and there were no rules and regulations for her. She could do no wrong and would have fits of shouting and stomping if she didn't get her way. Flats seem to be made of cardboard here as you can hear everything that happens in the other flats as though we were in the same one. As in most Italian families, the children rule the roost. There are no family rules, and they can disturb the neighbours to their heart's content as the parents can see no wrong. Most children do not want to go to bed when they should, even if that means being tired for school the next morning, and this little madam was no exception.

She would play football in the house or have one of her screaming fits very often till two in the morning. The father would leave it to his wife to take control and put up the volume on the TV in the bedroom where he was already in bed. This, of course, was directly underneath me, and there was no possibility of sleeping. When I asked them politely to try and be a little more respectful, they looked at me as though I were a Martian, and when things continued one night, I took a broom and banged it continually on the floor to make them stop. The next day, it seemed that I had done something really dreadful. I got an earful from the wife about how bad my behaviour was and how dare I make such a noise during the night. Me? And what about her daughter? In the end, she went on and on so much that I was actually beginning to believe that I was the one at fault!

As if this wasn't enough, with rude neighbours making a lot of noise at all times and other neighbours using my house as a waiting room, a family in the courtyard overlooking my bedroom decided to participate in the party of let's be rude and make life hell for others!

They were from the South and had just opened up a dry cleaning shop. The wife had a brother who was mentally handicapped and was usually in a special school. For some reason, they let him home. Like all Italians, they can't live far from all the family, so the dry cleaners were in one apartment and just over the road, the wife's parents with the problem son. With all due respect for this terrible problem, if the person is a danger to others, he should be kept under control, in my opinion. As usual, anything goes, and so the boy wandered around at his free will, insulting any female that walked by. It was bad enough for a woman to hear filthy insults, but he also molested little girls. He would follow them if they were outside on the grass, playing with friends. He would also follow them if their mothers were taking them to school or anywhere else. As long as the person was female, age didn't matter, and he would follow them, shouting his dirty language. Of course, nothing was done about it as the laws don't seem to be respected, and as for possible harm to another person, you can risk death before the police come out and do something about it, and then, of course, it's too late.

I'm sure there are some honest, hard-working officers of the law, but in this area, no one was to be found.

In the meantime, the other part of the family was just as bad in their own way. The wife would shout across the road to her parents rather than just going over to speak so everybody knew their business. The husband would get home from work and go into his hobby room. This was a few meters away from my bedroom and on the same level, so not only could I see him and he see into my room, but I could also hear him. His hobby was sculpturing, and he would take his hammer and be in his element every single evening and night until two o'clock in the morning. This went on for months and was a nightmare. No privacy and no sleep! I went to the police in the end to make a complaint.

There are different sorts of law enforcement officers here. For domestics and traffic disputes, they are called "Vigili Urbani" and would be the equivalent of our English Traffic Warden. The difference being that in Italy, even the Traffic Wardens carry a gun. Then there are the "Carabinieri," who are also in uniform and armed up to their teeth, carrying a Beretta and machine guns when doing spot checks. In fact, once, when I was with my friend Andy coming home from swimming, we were stopped at a random check point. There are always two officers, and while one asks for documents with his hand on his gun, the other is always on standby with his machine gun pointed at you. They take no chances, and quite honestly, it was rather frightening, and it was only a spot check!

The police who deal with tax evasion are called the "Guardia di Finanza" and are also in uniform and armed. There are other various categories, including the national police "Polizia di Stato," Polizia Penitenziaria, who are the prison officers and the Corpo Forestale, who are responsible for law enforcement in Italian national parks and forests.

In the beginning, it was quite frightening for me to see every type of officer armed and sometimes really heavily armed.

In England, I had been brought up to respect an officer in uniform, and I certainly didn't need to see a gun to behave myself in their presence. I was probably very lucky, though, living in the quiet Cambridge area and not in some of the London areas where kids really do have to put up with a lot of violence on the streets.

In the case of a domestic dispute, as was mine, I had to go to the Vigili Urbani, and to my surprise, the commander was very kind and understanding and promised to make a call. There are actually laws in Italy, and the one regarding disturbance is quite clear. You may work from 0800 till 2200 unless, of course, there is some sort of emergency and this covers private work in the home and so forth. The problem is people don't respect these laws, and as no one enforces them it is as though they don't exist.

The nice commander of the Vigili Urbani gave the family a telling-off, and he informed me that he had been round. The same evening, the hammering started again, and it was as if he had never been there. I complained again, and he went round again. This happened three times, and if a big guy in uniform had knocked on my door, I would have been scared stiff and apologised for the inconvenience caused, but of course, in Italy, it was different. The commander said he was sorry and that he could do nothing more and that, unfortunately, this particular family were very ignorant and not willing to abide by the law, and rather than make a fool of himself he considered his job done. He advised me to take it up a step and go to the Carabinieri, who were higher up and had more power.

The next day, I went to make my complaint to the other officials and that was even worse. I was shown into the office to speak to the commander in chief where I found a big fat guy reading a newspaper and drinking a coffee with his feet up on the table. Not once did he raise his eyes and say good morning and when I explained the situation, he said that people should use their own brains and realize that they were breaking the law and that he wasn't going to waste his time on such a pathetic incident when he had more important things to do – yes like reading the newspaper and drinking coffee I imagine! In the end, he basically accused me of wasting police time, and I was shown out. Well, that was a humiliating experience!

This is one of the problems here in that everyone knows they can get away with being selfish and doing what they want, even causing damage to others. In fact, when they chat with their peers and say that a police officer has been round and they have refused to follow the advice, they are considered to be one up and respected. They have broken the law and got away with it. That is something to be respected for and gain marks in their peer circle, and still, to this day, something I find difficult to accept.

The summer period was coming up, and everything shut down as usual for the month of August. People who cant afford to go on holiday take the opportunity of doing jobs in the house. The couple in a house over the street, only a few meters away, decided to redo the roof. I also couldn't afford a holiday but was looking forward to taking it easy and sitting on my balcony which looked right into their house. From the 1st of august till the 31st, they worked every day, including Sundays, hammering and nailing from 0800 till nearly midnight. Totally against the law, but who cares? That was my holiday and I could do nothing about it. There was no point in calling the police as I had already established and so I had to put up with it, shutting myself inside to avoid the noise, and with 38° heat outside, it wasn't very pleasant not to be able to open the windows.

Because it was summer, the restaurant just under our condominium was always full. They had a very pretty terrace garden, and of course, clients would prefer to eat outside. As there were not many restaurants or pizzerie in the area with outside accommodation, you can imagine the flow of people until the very late hours enjoying a bit of outdoor relaxation. This was all very well and a very pretty place, but of course, I could hear all sorts of private conversations that I really could have done without. As if this wasn't enough, Italians have the habit of chatting long after their meal outside and lots of groups after their dinner would form under my bedroom after leaving the restaurant, and in a drunken state would be even louder in their conversations.

Particularly at weekends, this tradition would go on sometimes till four in the morning, and it was driving me crazy.

As usual, I went down to the restaurant to have a word with the owner, but I was sent packing almost immediately. He said that once his clients were out of his premises, what they did and how much disturbance they caused was none of his business, nor did he care.

Well, thanks for that! It seems I am doomed to live in a world of noise and disrespect.

And by the way, the Germans also think along these lines. You should see the German tourists when they come to Italy. They love it and behave as if they are in a fantasy land. In Germany, the Germans are respectful, law-abiding citizens, but when they come to Italy, they can let their hair down, and that's exactly what they do. Coming from a rather oppressive rules and regulations situation, they see Italy as a place where rules don't exist, and who can blame them? They want a bit of freedom from the rigidity they have in their own country. They themselves become noisy, not very law-abiding citizens in what they consider a sort of Toy-land. If there are no rules for Italians, then why should a foreigner be afraid to have a good time? Just because he is a foreigner is an even bigger immunity as the police are not going to give them a telling off when, in a week or so, they will be back in their own country.

Getting away from the small anecdote and back to the flat, the noise problem did not end here. There was also a church just across the road, and the priest was also a law unto himself. The bells were not real bells but a recording which he would put on every quarter of an hour from 06.00 hours everyday. It was torture and made no sense whatsoever. In this day and age, everyone has a watch, and we don't need to be advised as to what time it is by his stupid bells. I thought that priests had a vocation to help people, not to torture them, but they wouldn't listen to reason. I wrote a letter to the diocese complaining about this exaggeration, and a very kind lady actually wrote back, which was strange. She was very understanding and explained what I already suspected, and that was that priests do exactly what they like as they feel important and will not listen to reason, so unfortunately, there was nothing she could do.

One night after two in the morning, when the sculptor guy had finally gone to bed, I thought that I could now get some kip for myself. However, just when I thought everything had finally quietened down, I started hearing some strange noises. I looked out of the window and saw some movement in the dark on the property beneath my flat. I also saw someone with a torch, and obviously, the first thing that came to mind was that there was a thief on the premises.

Even though I had been treated abominably by the law, I still thought I should do my citizen's duty and report what was going on to the police. I telephoned the emergency number and told them of my suspicions. The officer who answered, once having the address of where possibly a theft was in progress, started to get on his high horse and was extremely rude. He said that they were firemen who had been called out for a possible gas leak and were checking the premises. He then said that before I start wasting police time in the future I should get informed before making such calls! I couldn't believe it and asked him just how I was supposed to know that it wasn't a robber or something else and that I should have been thanked for doing my duty. He then went into a rage, and I really thought that I was going to end up getting reported for wasting police time and so I put the phone down on him. I made my decision in that instant to never ever help the police again, whatever should happen. Even if I am a witness to something, I must do what all the Italians do, and that is don't see, don't hear, don't talk. Just mind my own business. It really is much safer!

This sort of thing went on and on, so with the bells, the hammering of sculpture man and playing football and kangaroo jumping till two in the morning underneath me, plus the nosey neighbours treating my house like a waiting room, I decided I would have to move.

CHAPTER 22

I had put up with all the bad manners for so long, and not sleeping made life unbearable. I had been working for a few years with a consultancy firm and had managed to work my way up a bit with a better wage and more interesting work. I was a personal assistant to three of the deputy managers, two of which were very nice and easy to work with. The third unfortunately was a real pig head and expected me to do all sorts of personal favours like doing his shopping and going to the laundry. He would work in a small team on a project with other consultants and then take the credit for work the others had done.

He was literally hated by all, myself included! It was a real rat race atmosphere and they were all too quick to stab in the back and make a name for themselves. I hated this atmosphere and usually kept myself to myself and just made sure my deadlines were met. Of course this didn't go down very well and soon enough I was being isolated by pathetic little secretaries who would snob me or make silly comments about me not having designer clothes or shoes and not going out in the evening after work with them. I said that I preferred to get home to my husband, and as long as my work load was under control, they had no business telling me how to organise my spare time.

Some of their events, however, I just couldn't get out of, so dinners and weekends away were obligatory. The firm was doing well and had money to spend and they organised work weekends. One of these was in Ischia. Travel and hotel were paid for, and although there were work meetings, there was also free time to visit the island. Also our significant others were invited, which was nice. Faby seemed to get on well with my colleagues as he had a way with people, and so although he was from a different working world at the beginning, all was fine.

During my years with this firm, I made just one friend. He was gay and we got on really well. It was the first time I had had a gay friend and he was better company than all of the rest of the snobs put together. As we were both on the administration side and not the high up consultants we spent a lot of time together through work and would also have our lunch breaks together. His English was brilliant so it was nice to be able to switch from one language to another and make jokes. Sometimes we would have to work really late to meet deadlines and so I would stay in Milan overnight with my new friend so that Faby didn't have to come all the way and fetch me as there was no way I was going to get the last underground at night to get home. In this way I met his companion who was also great and we had some fantastic evenings together. Both the boys were really good cooks so often we would just stay home and have a meal together. Other evenings they would take me to the gay clubs where they usually went for a drink. It was quite an experience and nice to go somewhere and find no man chatting me up or being insistent because I was female! I really enjoyed the few years we had together and when problems started in the company they were the only ones that stood by me.

We started getting bad vibes and phone calls from head office in America asking strange questions, and it wasn't long before we realised that something wasn't right. This was happening all over again. The already rich bosses with their huge wage was not enough and yet again the regular office workers were going to pay the consequences. The office was not going to shut down completely but they were going to try and get rid of most people so that a new staff would come in and not know about the discrepancies. That is when the mobbing started. There were a couple of favorite secretaries who were given instructions by the bosses to start a mobbing tactic. If people were put under stress and left of their own accord then the company would not be liable to pay a golden handshake or any other offer to incite people to leave. It was disgusting how these two bootlicking secretaries felt in their realm and started putting people against each other or as in my case when I walked into a room a complete silence would fall. This was not the only tactic used as they would spread lies about my work so that I would get called for a fake telling off.

Of course I could always prove that they were lies as I had copies of my work but they were hoping that the stress would be too much and I would leave of my own accord. They had already succeeding in booting out the receptionist poor thing. They put her under a lot of pressure and offered her a hand out to quicken up the procedure. I have never seen such nastiness and false people in all my life, except of course for my husband's family who were on the same level. I don't think anyone in the end can endure such mobbing and it is always your word against their's and they know it. After several months of endurance, my friend and I decided take sick leave. I actually was sick after all this but we sought the advice of a lawyer and a union representative. The guy from the union was very understanding having seen this sort of behaviour many a time and knew what we were going through. They even harassed us on sick leave making up all sorts of things and after many months they found a way to sack both myself and my friend and others too, but it was only my friend and I who stuck together to try and fight the situation. The union guy advised us to go back to the lawyer and sue the company for unfair dismissal which is what we did. This was the first time I had had anything to do with lawyers in a situation like this. I had worked with a legal firm in the past but that was working for them, now the situation was different and I started getting a taste of things to come.

The lawyer was obnoxious, not at all helpful and kept telling my friend and I that we had no hope whatsoever of going against a big international firm. Of course we were right, we had been mobbed and sacked unfairly but who cares he said, thats how things go here! I was furious and reported his behaviour to the union guy and insisted he go ahead with the case and that is what happened. My friend after a few months gave up hope but I went ahead also on his behalf. I went to the meetings when the union guy called and we spoke to the lawyer and continually insisted that he pursue the case. The lawyer said that it was useless but he would do his job and put in the documents necessary to explain our case. I had to see him now and again for clarifications and the months went by. Every time I saw him he would ask if I wanted to give up as he wasn't really interested in following this case but every time I told him to get on with his job as I was going through with it. Months went by, a year went by and I'd more or less forgotten about it when one day I got summoned to go to court.

When I got there, I found my friend, who had also been summoned and who I hadn't seen in a while. There was one of the bosses present from the company and he didn't look pleased at all so I ignored him. Then the union guy came to greet me and told me that we were seeing a judge who had looked into our case and was going to talk to us and make a decision.

The courthouse in Milan is frightening. Its huge like a labyrinth. You get lost and indications are not helpful. Everyone is running about, there are armed police and such a hustle and bustle it is overwhelming. Thank goodness our union rep came looking for me otherwise I'd probably still be wandering around there today!

We went into a small office where the judge was sitting at his desk in plain clothes. No big court or anything strange, just a chat and a few questions about the treatment I had received from my former colleagues.

To my immense surprise, the judge was very human and understanding and said that we had, in fact, been treated very wrongly and that the maximum penalty for the company was to pay a whole year's wage to the wronged party, and that was exactly what he was going to do. Ok, it wasn't millions, but to be told that we were right was a huge satisfaction. Our lawyer couldn't believe it and stormed out. No apologies from him about his behaviour and his constant telling us that we didn't have a hope. His advice had been proved wrong and that was embarrassing for him so he just left! He should have been happy because now his invoice would be paid by the company but he was obnoxious from beginning to end. In the future I was going to have more to do with lawyers like him and it would seem that they really are all the same over here. However that's for later!

With my payout, I was able to extinguish the mortgage on my flat, and as I was now working from home doing translations and the money wasn't as good as my previous wage, it was a huge help. My friend couldn't believe it and thanked me for having battled and fought in his place while he had given up long ago.

Now my flat was paid for, I could finally put it up for sale and get something similar in a more peaceful area, hopefully. My work from home was for his companion, who had become my boss, and it kept us in touch even though we saw a lot less of each other. Unfortunately they were having problems as a couple at this time and separated much to my dismay. His companion found someone else who was not to our liking at all.

This country seems to be divided into two countries really, the North and the South. This is because the mentality is so different that it could be considered two different Italy's. My boss cum friend's new boyfriend was from Sicily and the problems started. Although the guy had lived in the North for quite a while his sense of jealousy, possessive and commanding nature had never left him. He started ruling the roost and laying down the law. So much so that although I was working for his companion and earning my wage honestly he saw that as a threat. Obviously being female I was no threat whatsoever in that sense, it was the fact that I was working for him and getting a wage that he would have preferred to have in his pocket. He made so much fuss that my friend had to tell me that he couldn't give me work anymore so as to not create problems with his new relationship. People will do anything for love and so I had to let it go. It was a huge disappointment both for me and his ex companion as we would have liked to remain in touch. My husband's sister in law was also from Sicily and her behaviour over the years was just the same. Interfering, jealous, and commanding my husband to hand over his wage to her to help maintain her family, things from another world! Their behaviour was so similar that they could have been relatives but of course it was just an unfortunate coincidence.

At this stage, I had no work and couldn't find anything else either, as I wasn't young enough anymore to be considered valid by anyone. Having paid off my mortgage and also going through bad health problems my husband decided it was better for me to stay at home and be a housewife.

At the time, I decided to give it a try, particularly as I wasn't fit to work anyway and with no mortgage to pay off, we could probably manage on one wage.

Famous last words!

At least now I would have the time to search for a new apartment, and as usual, Faby wasn't interested in helping at all. Thankfully my friend Andy was available and we fixed some appointments to go house hunting.

We found a place on the outskirts surrounded by fields and only a few houses, and it seemed very quiet. I put in an offer, and eventually after yet again many problems with the owners, we moved in. Once given the keys and checking over the place we found to our surprise that the couple had taken the kitchen door with them, the washbasin in the bathroom and many other things that should have been part of the flat! As usual the estate agency didn't want to know and the owners wouldn't listen to reason. Once again the lack of correctness was overwhelming. What seemed to be a lovely quiet corner was just going to be another hell hole once again. Just what is it with these Italians that they cannot appreciate peace and quiet?

There was an allotment just a few meters from my kitchen and never in a million years would I have thought it could have been a problem. However, every Sunday the owner would come about 7 am as if to work but by the time it got to 8 am the whole family was there setting the picnic table. They were southerners and loads of them too. The son brought a huge stereo and all sorts of wires to set it up as though it was a late night bar and of course the dance music at the highest possible volume was switched on. It was Sunday and the only day we liked to sleep in a bit. This was going to be impossible. I asked them very kindly if they could turn down the volume for at least another hour so we could sleep, but the father just looked at me and then went to the stereo to turn it up even more. Even if I live to be one hundred in this country I will never understand their need to be surrounded by noise!

Of course, that wasn't the only problem, was it? I couldn't have been lucky with peaceful neighbours, could I? We are in Italy, and that doesn't happen! I had another loud-mouthed family right next door. Wonderful, I have moved to find myself in an even worse situation.

The wife was a real screamer and would have to announce to the world when she left at 7 in the morning and when she got back with the kids in the evening. She would swear at the poor things so loudly that I'm sure they could hear her in the next village. That not being sufficient, she would continue her roaring all evening until the children went to bed, which, of course, here is very late. Faby would not hear of moving again, and I was doomed to live in the midst of noise and rudeness even though we were in the countryside.

In the first few years, my father had helped Faby economically so he could set up his own business. Now, with him working for himself and all the time he spent with his family, I was basically on my own in an even worse situation. Great, it's a never-ending story!

CHAPTER 23

During these years, my only outlet was getting away to Germany. I had packed my bags on the verge OF leaving a hopeless marriage so many times that I really can't remember. Every time I made up my mind Faby would seem so generally upset and sad that I felt awful. I didn't know that it was just for show and his usual keeping up appearances. I knew that it wasn't going to work as his family had too much of a hold and were ruining both our lives. Unfortunately he didn't see it that way and as the niece was growing up he only had eyes for her. As I was now a housewife with no income it made the situation even harder and I realised I should have left while still in the job market. However we seemed to find the solution with me going to Germany. He could tell his family that I was there for studies or for work. It really didn't matter to me what he told them as long as I could get out finally. It seemed that we had reached a taciturn agreement.

With our coming and going from the Oktober Fest over the years, I had always tried to insert other places of interest during the trips, and I had come to love Germany.

Although the Oktober Fest is great fun, I was beginning to get fed up of looking after a group of lads who just got drunk. I had to translate and then get them back to the hotel in the evening in one piece instead of dividing the day with cultural visits, so finally getting them to see sense and visiting some other parts of Germany was a great step forward.

On one occasion, I discovered a beautiful historical town in the Middle Franconia region of Bavaria. It was a little jewel and offered everything within walking distance to museums, shops, churches and musical concerts. Even Faby's friends loved the place and we started having more short holidays there rather than going to the beer festival thankfully.

Unfortunately, every time we went, his friends had to tag along, and we never had a weekend just to ourselves. It was even noticed by the friends we had made in the small town and each time we had an invite somewhere I would turn up on my own as he was doing a round of the bars with his friends. I really did feel a single to all effects now and had to work at getting my life back. As I was a housewife and had more time for myself I decided to start studying again.

The summers in Milan were unbearable so I started to do language courses in Germany to get away from the heat. It gave me a chance to get away from his awful family with the excuse that I wasn't in the country. Every summer his brother would go on holiday no matter what which meant that my husband would have to stay around to look after his mother. She was still pretty fit and didn't need looking after but her pressure on him made it impossible to leave. Of course his brother couldn't give a damn. We couldn't go to England ourselves for a holiday which meant either I went off on my own or I was stuck in the house all day with air conditioning on and bored out of my mind while he went off to work and spent the rest of his time with the evil witch. The climate was so much better in Germany and the university course was good in the beginning. I had begun my new path with a view to eventually leaving Italy altogether and even better, never to see his nasty family again!

During the years, my stays got longer and longer and I was studying hard, trying to master a difficult language.

You would have thought that after a month away from each other, he would have been pleased to see me again and come over to fetch me on his own being a good excuse to have a weekend and get away from bossy mother. But each time my course finished and it was time to go back to Italy he would turn up with his friends or his pushy little niece. Once he came to pick me up and not only were his friends there and I had to rush around finding rooms for them but he had also brought the kid with him without telling me or even asking me if I liked the idea. There she was, all over him, possessive as usual, and what was worse he told me that she had to sleep in my digs that I had rented for the duration of the course. I had a fit. He knew how much I detested family interference and that is why he brought her without telling me.

So, no privacy and she had to kip down with me otherwise we would have had to pay out of our own pocket because of course his brother had not provided her expenses. It was hard enough finding the money each year for my course, but it was in the hope that another language would permit me to find work again and we certainly shouldn't be wasting hard earned cash on her. Even his friends said that he was out of order this time doing such a thing behind my back and in view of my reaction it certainly didn't make for a comfortable weekend. It was too late, she was there so we would have to make the best of it. So after not seeing my husband for a month we had the weekend in the company of his friends and little madam. They walked around the town hand in hand just like two little love birds and I would be invisible to all. It was unbelievable the complete lack of sensitivity. Of course she was in her element with my husband all to herself and rubbing it in every minute that went by giving me sly little looks when he wasn't looking. He knew how I felt about his scrounging family so this certainly didn't make things easier.

The weekend passed, and I couldn't wait to get home and get rid of her Cheshire cat face. You could cut the air with a knife, that was the atmosphere during the weekend, and he never apologised.

After that particular incident, he would start coming home from work really late and was at her beck and call. His excuses were lame and the little madam did everything she could to have him running about for her. The same thing was happening with the rest of the family too, always asking for money for something or other. I tried to put my foot down about the few things I had knowledge of but he was so scared of his family and so attached to appearances that he would prefer not to tell me anything so that he could give them everything they wanted at our expense.

Sometimes, I would try to make an effort to keep an equilibrium, and with traditional events like Christmas and Easter, I would be put under so much pressure to do the right thing and cook a meal, etc, that I would give in. It was always very trying and every time the girl was in my house she would not hesitate to tell me how much she would like to live in my house with my husband.

I begged him to have a word with the girl and her mother, as this was an obsession, and she was obviously unstable. For me this behaviour just wasn't normal and besides being very interfering I found it somewhat disturbing. I got a mouthful of abuse and was told to leave his family out of things and that it was NONE of my business. How strange that it is my business when I have to cook for them and have them in my house but anything else including the scrounging and bad manners is something that doesn't concern me!

I tried to reason with the mother from time to time and told her that the interference in my marriage was just not acceptable and that her daughter must be kept under control. That did no good at all and was of no surprise when the woman wouldn't listen. I just received a mouthful of abusive language and told to leave her daughter alone.

Whatever she wanted she would get and her father would not miss a week without some sob story or other as to why he needed money. I only got to know about a few of the mishaps by chance, all the rest of their devious actions came out much later.

CHAPTER 24

I had been going to Germany for so many years that I had really fallen in love with the country and with one small historical town in particular. I was hoping to get a seasonal job there in the summer to be able to support myself and was working hard with my studies. There was no point in staying in Italy in the summer as my husband was either working or with family and friends and a bit of extra money would be helpful and as my objective was eventually to live there permanently this was the start I imagined.

I had found out in the meantime that I couldn't have children, and Faby would not hear of adopting a child. At this point I was obviously a disgrace for his mother and made things even more difficult so my German idea kept getting stronger and stronger.

One of the outings I had organised in the past was a few days on what is called the Romantic Road, starting from the south of Germany in Füssen to the north in Würzburg. The first stop was the beautiful fairy tale castle of Neuschwanstein which nearly everyone knows due to its typical shape seen as an outline at the beginning of Walt Disney films. The road took us through wonderful towns and villages combining historic cities and medieval walled towns, all quite breathtaking.

One of the small historic towns, in particular, left me speechless with its beauty, and it was love at first sight for me. A town with a charm that would be my home for a while.

A mutual friend of ours knew how strongly I felt about the idea and also knew the family situation that I had to deal with and came up with the idea that would be a big help to me. He was toying with the idea of making an investment, but buying a house and then renting it, particularly in Italy, was not a good idea. Once you have a person in your house renting it is very difficult if not impossible to get rid of them once the contract has ended. Even though legally a contract ends and the people should leave the premises most of them refuse to do so and to get a court order to get them out can take years and sometimes a lifetime. Nothing seems to work here and it is widely known that the laws and not made to be respected, hence his idea of buying a flat in Germany where I could live and look after the place for him knowing that if he wanted the place for himself or wanted to sell he would have no problems with me leaving if he so needed. It sounded fantastic and would mean that I would have no rent to pay and what I was able to earn from a possible summer job would be mine to keep.

The only problem was that I would have to manage everything in Germany, from flat hunting to the contracts. Our friend was in a difficult situation looking after his infirm mother which meant he was not free to oversee all the procedures in Germany. We agreed that as I was so often over there for my studies I could cope with all the things to do myself. I managed to find a place that was a really good price but needed a lot doing to it to be able to live in it. He agreed and gave me a budget to work on which covered the price of the flat and some extra to do it up to make it liveable.

I couldn't believe my luck. With only my husband's wage and all the scrounging from his family, no way could we have ever afforded a holiday home, so it really did seem like a miracle.

I met up with the estate agency, and everything seemed to be going smoothly. I worked out a budget of the things necessary like a new bathroom and kitchen which were in a terrible state. I don't think I have ever seen such filth. The motorway toilets were cleaner. How can anyone live in such a state without cleaning now and again! The lady who lived in the flat didn't seem to see the dirt she was living in and had really let the place go so some immediate work would have to be done just to be able to have the essentials at the beginning.

I had always had the impression that Germany was an efficient country, and on the face of things, that's how it seemed, but it is only when you start living in a place that reality hits you as always.

Things were going slowly and then wrong. After a few months I got a call to say there would be a meeting with the owner and the estate agency and wondered what was going on.

Apparently, the owner had some problems and would have to wait two years to sell the house, also the lady who was renting at the time had refused to leave the flat. I was very tempted to leave the whole situation and start looking for somewhere else but he proposed what seemed a good idea at the time, and that was for me to rent in the meantime and at the end of the two years that sum would be taken off the price of the house and I could consider it already mine. It seemed a fair proposal leaving the house price as it was but the next problem was the renter who wanted a sum of money to leave the place otherwise she would cause trouble. I thought these things only happened in Italy so this was a bit of a surprise.

Apparently people who rent in Germany have a lot of protection from the state and it is very hard to get them out even with a contract that specifies the leaving date however, it was proposed to go half and half with the sum she wanted. As the price of the flat was advantageous I agreed rather unwillingly but it meant that we could start work soon and the next summer holidays would be free rather than having to pay for a hotel.

The procedure to get all the paperwork done was slow, and I was very surprised at how snail-like they were. However, we got there in the end signing a contract with the exclusive right to purchase the flat in two years time at the agreed price .

I had a tight budget, and prices were very high in Germany, much more so than in Italy so Faby proposed to do the work himself with the help of a plumber friend from Italy and assured me that this would mean huge savings. What could I say, it seemed a fair offer and he was very persuasive as usual. The friend who was investing in this project also agreed having the impression that my husband was competent and that in fact would be a big savings.

Various materials were purchased in Italy, costing less and he brought them over to Germany in his work van. Little by little as work commenced all sorts of problems started to arise and he realised that the place was really in a bad state. Perfectionist as he is he wanted to do things properly but it would need more money and more help from Italy. I was very against this saying that at this stage it was better to get labour from the area and just do what was absolutely necessary and the rest we could do a little at a time when possible. He started to go over my head and organise with his friends completely against my advice. He engaged a bricklayer friend of his to come over and re-do the bathroom saying that he could get the tiles and other material in Italy through him at half the price. I was very much against this as we would have to pay not only his time but also board and lodgings in Germany and at the end of the day would cost less paying a labourer on the spot without hotel and food. Of course rows started up as he said he knew best and it was none of my business, the usual phrases and insults when he wanted to do things his way. It was beginning to get out of hand and very frustrating. So much time had already been lost due to the German end being so slow with getting things agreed upon and if we wanted the place to be ready by the summer then we would have to get a move on. He organised a date for materials to be delivered and plumber and bricklayer to take holiday time from their jobs so we would have a week working together.

It was already putting us way behind schedule waiting for the guys in Italy to get time off when we could have had someone already working from the area, but when the time finally came to set off, yet another setback came along. The bricklayer who had suffered a leg injury decided on the very same day that we should have been leaving that perhaps he ought to go to the ER. Why couldn't he have done it weeks ago? Because of his stupidity our leaving date had to be put off. I was furious and told Faby we should get someone from the area to do the work so as not to be held back. His friend had not been fair. I was sorry for his injury but business is business and I had deadlines to meet. This provoked more rows but Faby had promised work to the guy and wanted to keep his promise. My argument on the other hand was that his friend was not respecting our deadlines. I had not approved of him coming in the first place and he should have sorted his health problems out earlier if he wanted the work. No can do.

Everything was put off and who knows when the plumber can get time off again, Faby's friend was putting us in a difficult situation and in fact we had to wait months before we could start off again. The flat was on the fourth floor with a lift for only the first two floors so, someone with an injury like the bricklayer friend would have huge difficulties getting up the other two floors. It just wasn't feasible. I had no say in the matter as usual and finally our leaving date came round again. Our meeting place was on the motorway for a coffee and to my surprise not only did the bricklayer turn up but he had brought his son with him as he wouldn't be able to do the stairs! This meant an extra room and food in the hotel for a person that would be doing basically nothing. I found out that Faby knew about this and yet again avoided telling me because he didn't have the heart to say no to his friend. I could see our budget fading away very quickly. Our plumber friend was also astounded and as furious as myself with this behaviour. There was nothing I could do at this stage and we were already so behind schedule that we started off on our travels.

It was a disaster. The son was useless and was always tired. After having lugged up materials a couple of times for his father he refused to do anything else. The father with his bad leg had difficulty bending to put the tiles on the floor and cut corners. The people in the restaurant where I had a tab for the workers lunch told me that the boy was going there for an aperitif and putting it on my tab. He was basically there for a free holiday and complaining at how he didn't like the place. They also told me that the bricklayer complained constantly that the food was not how his wife would make it! For heavens sake! You wanted the work, you've put us all behind and now all you can think about is that the food is not how your wife makes it? Of course it's not, we're in Germany but that doesn't mean to say the food is not good here, it's just different! Italians with their food habits again!

My husband would not listen to reason, what a surprise, and was embarrassed about the whole situation and decided to do nothing about it as the guy was his friend. Things were not going according to plan!

It was too late now, and money had been spent, so we had to go ahead with whatever.

Faby would go back and forth from Italy to Germany and was exhausted but still wouldn't listen to reason. During this time his family of course couldn't mind their own business and wanted continual updates as to what was happening. They were under the misconception that he was buying the flat as I found out later and he so wanted the approval of his niece he lied to make himself important to her. I didn't think much of it at the time as usual thinking it was a misunderstanding but the niece as usual couldn't bear the thought of my husband being far away and not available for her and I got bombarded with texts asking for a free holiday and the use of the flat. It was absolutely impossible to live there yet with all the renovation work still to do and if it had been ready I would have been there saving on hotel fees and certainly not giving free holidays at my expense to an interfering, jumped up kid. Even after explaining to the girl what the situation was she would not believe me and said she had the right to use the flat! Just who does she think she is with all this bossing about and laying the law down. This went on for months and got to be a real harassment. Faby wanted to bring her over each time but I put my foot down asking who would pay the hotel and of course the answer was always the same. His brother expected us to pay. What a scrounger! We were all working hard at the time and would not be possible in any case for us to stop working so that she could be taken around like a princess and interfere with our already late schedule.

Of course that didn't go down very well but at least this time I got my way. We were already over budget because of his insistence of bringing his friends from Italy to work. The only one I don't regret paying for is the plumber who really did work his butt off and do an excellent job. It still would have cost me less with someone on site but he was worth the money. As for the other two, father and son, never again! Another right pair of scroungers!

My husband also had his work in Italy but had taken on this ridiculous commitment and had to organise his work in Italy and days off to go to Germany. It was too much but he wouldn't change his mind and later on it came to light that he was doing it not for me but for that little madam of his niece. Yet again his family poking their noses into things that don't concern them. He was so preoccupied with making a good impression to his family that he was making promises that were not his to make.

No wonder the little madam was behaving like a princess. She thought she was onto a good thing with a sugar daddy buying her a holiday home, and no wonder she treated me like dirt, thinking she was the one with rights to my husband, and in fact, that is how it was!

Things were really getting out of hand, but when Faby said that he wanted to do things properly and he would make up for going over the budget by selling a little flat that had been left to him by his Aunt I believed him. He had such a way of making the impossible seem possible and such a bootlicker that I always believed him. If this was the case then we would be able to get back on budget and not let our friend down by not managing the situation properly, and so it was decided.

The little madam of his niece was still such a pain in the neck and was constantly hassling both him and myself, and in the end, I had to get really angry and tell him enough was enough that I didn't want her there under any circumstances. It was a one bedroomed flat for us and I would be using it to get a seasonal job and earn a bit of money and had no time for her, my program did not include her in any way.

At this stage, he went behind my back, as I found out later, but from that moment, as far as I was concerned, she wasn't mentioned again.

Due to his work in Italy, I would stay over by myself to get some work done on my own and although most things went according to plan, others did not. I did my best speaking in a foreign language but there were some times that I just couldn't make myself understood when it got to technical terms. The few German labourers that were engaged to do work in the flat would pretend not to understand and do things their way. When Faby came over to check on the work done he would flare up at me saying how useless I was and incompetent. Once I did find the courage to answer him back saying that if his german was better than mine then he should be here with the labourers and speak to them himself in german. That shut him up for about five short seconds then he would go off on another tangent with his complaints about me and how stupid I was. This was all working up to a huge row yet again because of his niece I found out. While I was in Germany and he back in Italy it was the perfect chance for little madam to have my husband all to herself and work her brain washing on him and she certainly wasn't going to miss that chance.

She wanted that holiday home, whatever the cost and would stop at nothing to get what she wanted. With her mother, the sister in law, behind her all the way I realised much too late what they were planning. On a couple of occasions with this to and fro going on one of Faby's part time helpers would accompany me to Germany and do some of the heavier work in the flat and he confirmed to me that she would be constantly telephoning him as soon as he left the house to go to work so that she could speak to him when I wasn't present. Little did she know that his worker was in the van with him and could hear the conversation which was obviously not in my favour.

This went on for the whole duration of work in the flat and the harassing texts trying to get around me too would be nonstop.

Christmas came around, and knowing that there would be the usual farce of having to make excuses not to go around to his family for lunch, he decided to spend his holiday period working in the flat. He took a couple of friends with him for help and left me behind alone over Christmas. I suppose it was better to be alone than with his family so I just accepted it. His family of course knew I was alone during this period and just ignored me. This was yet another confirmation about how they treated me. I told him hoping that he would open his eyes as to what sort of family he had. He was furious and blamed me, saying I wasn't the sort of person anyone could get on with! That was strange seeing how many friends I had made in Germany over the years and had even been invited to a wedding amongst other events so that affirmation really didn't stand up.

There was no way of making him see how they were using him and

I left him to his work.

He would never admit it but I'm sure he had a better Christmas working and celebrating with his friends than he would have done if he had been in Italy with his family.

He got back to Italy extremely angry and tired and this atmosphere went on for weeks. The day after he got back the landline rang and it was his niece. She wanted to know how I was! I had a fit. Ten days alone over the holiday period and not a word to see if I was dead or alive and now what a coincidence, my husband gets home and I receive a phone call. Does she really think I'm that stupid?

The kid was now in her 20s and this sort of behaviour at this age should not be happening. It really is incredible how this girl thinks that no one will notice how crafty she is and take things AT face value. This provoked another huge row as no one likes to be made fun of and particularly by a tiny little upstart like her who thinks that she is the worlds biggest brain and not modest with it either.

Over the next few weeks, I honestly don't know what she and her family were saying. The amount of brainwashing they were doing on my husband, the result was catastrophic. After having begged him for the millionth time to defend me at least a bit and stop letting them treat me so badly, he came home and dropped the bombshell.

He said that it was all over because that was what his niece wanted and that the next day, he would be taking me to Germany as he needed to be alone for a while. I thought it was a joke in very bad taste and the next day we set off with me thinking he wanted to show me the work done in the flat.

CHAPTER 25

When we arrived in Germany, I saw that the flat was empty. The new bathroom was functioning and the kitchen seemed to be set and ready. The flooring had been done months before, which I had already seen and so now furniture needed to be bought.

To my amazement he said that he was leaving me there in the flat and I would have to make a new life for myself. I was so flabbergasted that I didn't react. I couldn't come to terms with what was going on and thought he was joking.

He said that his niece was the most important person in his life, always had been and that I was absolutely nothing to him and never had been.

After hearing something like that, and after having spent the last twenty-five years of my life with him, putting up with the continual nastiness from his family just for him, I went into a sort of shock mode and just stood there like an idiot.

He left me in that state and went back to Italy as if everything was fine and normal.

I tried to phone him once I had recovered a bit, but he said that as I had refused to let little Madam live with me in the flat during the period in which we were working, then it was all over, and he would let me stay there so I had a roof over my head but the rest was up to me. First of all the flat was not his to make this decision as it belonged to our mutual friend and was supposed to be a holiday home for the three of us and nothing to do with his family. Our friend, who was really more of my friend, had also made it quite clear that he wasn't doing this for Faby's family but more for me. He had always known how they treated me and didn't want them taking advantage. He couldn't have been more clear on the subject.

Secondly, because of the strange contract we had and the fact that the place would have been bought in the future, it was still being rented, so even my friend was not yet the owner. All these thoughts and problems would have to wait for the moment as I was stuck in Germany without a penny and with no job, and in any case, these were projects that were supposed to be considered later on in the year in the summer period. It was February, which meant the locals were all shut and had their holidays, as the rest of the year was very busy for them. Just one friend who had a hotel kept it open and, with a skeleton staff, worked the slack period. I didn't know what to do, so I went over to the hotel just to have some company and tell them what was going on. They were all shocked as much as I was, as he had always given the impression of being a nice guy, but the facts were clear. The manager of the hotel said she had been through a rough patch years ago with a young child to look after as well, and her husband had thrown her out, and she had to start again. With all her problems, she did have a job, though and managed to get through, but without a penny, how do you start again? In any case I had a house in Italy for which I had paid the most part with my wage when I did have a job, so no way was he going to take that from me. That was easier said than done. The next few days were hell, and I had a real breakdown. My small circle of friends were really good to me and one of the guys took me to the doctors on one of the days that I could hardly stand on my feet. I couldn't sleep, and everything was turning around.

After a few days, I called my one and only friend in Italy and told him what was going on. He was also completely taken by surprise but at the same time pleased as he had seen the way I had been treated and told me to try and take it in a positive way, but of course, that was too difficult at the time. I also spoke to a lawyer acquaintance that I had known for years and who had been kind to me when I first came to Italy. She said that I must get back to Italy and sort things out and that he had no right whatsoever to claim everything I had for his family and dump me in a foreign country. My friend allowed me to use his account in Germany so that I could buy food from the supermarket and manage to live during the next few weeks. My other friend at the hotel told me to give my husband time and let him have some peace as he was obviously having a nervous breakdown, so I was torn between her advice and the advice of the lawyer, who said I should get back as soon as possible.

After a couple of days, Faby's sister-in-law started calling. She had obviously been told all sorts of lies, as usual, and for the next week, I got continual hate calls, which were very upsetting. I was in Germany alone and in an empty flat, which was already depressing. He had left me in a terrible state, and now these phone calls.

She was insulting and abusive, and I told her for the thousandth time that she should have kept her daughter on a leash and stopped her from interfering with my marriage. That brought on another avalanche of insults, and I was told that I should not dare to speak about her daughter and that the little madam had a very special relationship with my husband and always had done and it was none of my business. Well, just how can that be, as I am his wife? According to his family, nothing is ever my business, and how can a mother purposely push her own daughter into breaking up a marriage?

Listening to this woman's calls was yet another shock. She had been told that the flat in Germany where I was at that moment had been bought by my husband. This, of course, was not true, but she was adamant about it and besides, she had been told that the flat was specifically for little madam, her daughter, so no wonder she wanted me out. More lies. Now I know why she was so approving of her daughter taking away my husband, all for what they were convinced of gaining. If the situation hadn't been so horrible for me, I would have felt sad for them, but when I tried to explain that the flat was not ours at all, she would not have heard of it and called me a liar.

In the end, I let it go, realising you cannot reason with a person who is convinced of something completely the opposite. In any case, it was none of her business, and if she wanted to dream that the holiday home would be her daughter's very shortly, then let her dream on. It was at least a confirmation to me that I was not paranoid and that all my suspicions of them wanting me out were true and the sad thing was that it was all for money and assets that we just didn't have! So many lies were being discovered. Why oh why did he lie, not only to me, his wife, which was unforgivable, but evidently he had been lying to his own family as well just to feel important. That sort of thing catches up with you sooner or later, so why do it?

She went on and on with her ravings, and I was shocked that the situation was even more critical than I thought. She said it was her behind all the economic decisions that my husband took and that his wage was hers to manage, and our income was none of my business! She said I was just a parasite taking away an income that was rightfully her daughter's as I had no children!

She also let it slip that it was her who had insisted that Faby pay for the flat where his mother was living. His parents had been renting the place forever, but when the owner of the condominium died, the heirs decided to sell everything off. This meant no more renting but buy or get out.

I suggested that they move into another flat, and what their pension didn't cover, the two brothers should go fifty-fifty. Shock, horror that would mean the brother would have to fork out a few quid for his own mother. No way!

In fact, the sister-in-law had insisted they Faby take care of everything as usual, and he did, again behind my back.

This was a huge decision to make, and it should have been discussed with me, certainly not decided together with his sister in law. The bitchy woman was a devil. She brought up so many nasty points of how she had been commanding my husband and his wage for years behind my back and that I was an outsider with no right to be part of the family. I didn't actually want to be part of the family and hadn't since day one so that was no problem but the other horrid things she would go on about were very hurtful. The fact that I couldn't have children was according to her my fault. I had asked my husband years ago if we could think about adopting a child but his response was that he didn't want anyone else's children and our life was fine just the way it was.

This was evidently another lie as he had taken on the responsibility of his niece right from day one and his sister in law told him that as I had no children it was his precise duty to maintain her children and in particular the oldest one. This was all double dutch to me and I couldn't see how any of this was her business and what a cheek to be commanding my husband's wage behind my back amongst all things. She was evil, it's as simple as that. Digging the knife in deeper and deeper making me feel at fault for not being able to have children. She would not agree to my point of view that it was not up to us to fork out for her nor should she be disrespectful to me making decisions with my husband behind my back. There was no way of reasoning with her. She was completely convinced that her way was the right way. I had suspected for years that they had been poking their noses into my personal life but every time I asked for explanations I was brutally told to mind my own business. I would have thought that our income is my business but whenever I tried to get information out of Faby a row would start and I never got anywhere. He would always make up something plausible or be very abusive and I would never get an honest answer.

It finally dawned on me that although this family was not a mafia family and in no way was connected to the mafia, unfortunately, her upbringing had given her the very same mentality. She had become the "kingpin" in the family, and that is the Boss. I quote:

A mob boss, crime lord, Don or kingpin is a person in charge of a **criminal organization.** A boss typically has absolute or near-absolute control over his subordinates, is greatly feared by his subordinates for his ruthlessness and willingness to take lives in order to exert his influence, and profits from the criminal endeavours in which his organisation engages.

The boss in the **Sicilian** and **American Mafia** is the head of the **crime family** and the top decision-maker.

Although she was not in a criminal organisation, she was, in my opinion an immoral criminal using my funds to support her own family without my knowledge up to that point and definitely the top decision maker. Taking lives was also not her style in the literal sense, however, she was and evidently had been taking my life in a certain sense according to her account of things and as the days went by she did her best to drive me to suicide with her hateful and abusive calls. That is how bad the calls were until I decided to block her number so that I would not have to listen to all the awful things she had to say.

As you can see from the definition quoted, apart from killing people or getting someone to do it for her, she is a match to the definition, and my husband just wasn't man enough to stand up to her and fight for his marriage.

After these horribly upsetting calls, some of the jigsaw started to come together and looking back I now realise why we had such a hard time. I should have been more alert and not so trusting but it's so easy to say after the fact.

Even though he was paying her since day one and giving his niece a life of a princess behind my back the real problems started when I stopped working. I found out afterwards when I had to get a lawyer and they started investigating that the debts started to accumulate from the day I lost my job.

Instead of standing up to his sister-in-law and saying that the payouts had to stop as I was now unemployed, he was too afraid of her. His abnormal attachment to appearances didn't help. He desperately wanted to make them believe he was a huge success as a business man and hence the lies. What a wally! Just who had I married?

CHAPTER 26

I had to wait a month before he came and picked me up again after insisting heavily and also telling him that Andy was going to let me have the money to buy a ticket to get home in any case, so I was coming back to my home, whatever.

During these weeks, Andy was very supportive and tried to keep my spirits up, but at the same time, he thought that he had better update me on things. Given the situation and the way I had been abandoned he told me that the truth must be told. A couple of years ago Faby had called him saying he was in a desperate situation and needed a loan. Andy said that he should talk to me about it and explain what was going on but Faby refused saying that he didn't want to worry me. Of course now we know that the money was for his family and the fact that his sister in law was claiming the whole of his wage he had no other choice but to get loans where he could to make ends meet. Because of his previously apparent honest reputation Andy agreed to give him a loan. It was a lot of money and I was furious that no-one had told me sooner. Andy said that he had been made to promise not to tell me and I said that it should have made him wary and questioned why but he was too kind and trusting and now the money had gone, disappeared without trace. This was just the beginning of surprises yet to come and I decided I would ask where the money had gone.

I got through the four weeks in Germany as best I could, and the day arrived for him to come and pick me up. After abandoning me like that there was no way I could live with him anymore and so I waited for the imminent telling off and the list of all my faults and how I would have to change if I wanted to go back to him. Little did he know that I had already made up my mind that I couldn't live with a liar. He was the one that should change his ways and for a start stand up to his family but I knew that was never going to happen as he had been brain washed from birth and was not going to change now.

He arrived, and we went for our evening meal where we would be in public and could avoid a row, I hoped. He started ranting as I imagined and I stopped him half way through saying I would agree to a separation. He didn't expect that at all and was shocked for a moment thinking that I would be waiting humbly for him to give me a list of changes to be made and become even more of a doormat for him. I also asked about the loan and why none of it had been paid back. He was furious saying that Andy had promised not to say anything. Under the circumstances I said he was right to inform me and why on earth had my own husband said nothing to me and what exactly was the money for? I only received the usual verbal, offensive abuse being told that nothing was any of my business. He was not the least bit upset about me agreeing to a separation but more annoyed about having failed the image that he wanted the world to see and that is a successful businessman with a normal life and a happy wife. It was all a load of crap and all he was interested in was appearances. My friend in the hotel also tried to talk to him about what was going on and he just insisted that it was all my fault, that his family were perfect and in no way were there money problems.

Who is he kidding? I thought to myself. Does he really believe what he is saying?

During this time, I had also spoken to my parents about the situation, and of course, they were astounded by his behaviour. I referred their questions to Faby and that brought on another round of abuse and I was accused of not asking his permission first to speak to my own parents! He wanted everything to go his way of course and was used to making all the decisions himself even for my own life and things were evidently not going to plan. According to him I should have stayed in Germany out of sight out of mind so he could be the hero in Italy saying how wonderful he had been to his wife when she had treated him so badly. He just wanted the appreciation of everyone for something that was completely untrue and with me out of the way he could have told people anything he liked and made a wonderful impression. Its all about appearances with him and always will be.

It was an awful dinner, as was to be expected, but at least the next day, I would be back in Italy and in my own home and perhaps be able to sort a few things out.

CHAPTER 27

The journey was terrible; the atmosphere was heavy, and I kept crying all the way. There was no reasoning with him and he was a complete bully.

We got back, and I shut myself in my room and waited for the next day when he would go to work and I could have some peace.

I started looking through the accounts and tried to find out exactly what the situation was and saw that the bank statements regarding the loan my friend had made to him were missing. If he is hiding that then there are going to be more surprises and that made me even more suspicious.

I found that in the month I had been away, Faby had taken advantage of being in the house alone, and all sorts of things were missing, but with what little I managed to recuperate, I made photocopies and tried to hide them. They might come in useful given the way things were going.

He had inadvertently left a letter from the bank on the desk, and upon opening it, I found, to my surprise, a threat to repossess my house as he hadn't been paying his part of the mortgage. Good grief what is happening?

He got home late in the evening as usual and went upstairs to have a shower.

He left his mobile phone in the kitchen where I was preparing the dinner. He usually left it there once home and would leave it on just in case an urgent call from clients came which did happen now and again

I had never ever checked his phone; it wasn't my style, and I had always completely trusted him. However, that particular evening, a text came through, and it was right in front of me as if by fate. I immediately saw a message from the little brat of a niece and given the situation I looked at it. I felt bad as I had never spied on him before but the nature of the message was very alarming so I read the whole thing. The kid had written him a love letter. I was disgusted.

At this point, I searched his history of emails and texts. To my amazement, the kid had been sending him all sorts of communications that, in other circumstances, I would have said he was having an affair, but being from his niece was extremely worrying.

I had always known that she was obsessed with him and had always tried to turn him against me but these messages were over the top completely.

This time, I couldn't let it go, and I wanted an explanation. During the years I had begged both him and the child's mother to knock some sense into her but of course I was insulted and told to mind my own business, the favorite saying from both of them as always. The kid was really not so much of a kid being now 25 years of age and so the situation was even more worrying as it was not an infatuation of a small child but a person who should now have enough intelligence and knowledge of life to realise that what she was doing was wrong.

During the years, I had tried to learn to live with their nastiness and interfering for Faby's sake, but little by little, I was beginning to realise that five against one gave me no chance and that I had never had any possibility in reality.

Now that some of the truth was out, he was getting scared and would not give any explanations. The only way for him to keep his secrets from me was to get rid of me hence his plan of dumping me in Germany. That hadn't worked out for him and quite rightly so as the house we were living in had been paid for with my wage and the remaining amount to be paid should now be paid off by his work as I was the one who had provided for both of us until now. However, that was not to be considered according to him and to hide all the evil from me he thought that dumping me yet again was his only way out to keep his secrets and keep face with his family.

He was nasty and accusing and did everything he could to make me feel at fault. For what, I really don't know as I had put up with so much for his sake all these years. Anyway, to cut a long story short he threw me out of my own house. His niece didn't even have the guts to be present but from what he told me it was all her idea and that was probably the only truth he has ever told me in all these years. She had never made any secret of her expectations to live in my house with my husband and her morbid obsession made her think she had the right to do just that. He told me that I had to go as little madam had decided that I could no longer be part of the family and that his alliance was solely to her! What sort of man is it that can't even make his own decision regarding his wife but has to be told by a little upstart what to do. I was dumbfounded. He went on and on about how important she was to him and that I had never been anything to him and lots more. He kicked me out in her name taking my house keys from me and thought I would disappear into nowhere never to be seen or heard of again. Really!

I was out on the streets with nothing. No home, no money, no job.

Thankfully he had let me keep my mobile phone and so I called my best friend and only friend in Italy and asked if he could help.

During my years as a housewife, Faby had isolated me little by little and refused to let me see the few friends I had as he preferred to be in the company of his own peers or family, so the fact that Andy had stood by me all this time was a miracle. He was also having family problems in that his mother was ill, and he had decided to look after her full-time. His father unfortunately had passed away and with the mother not being at all well he had decided to move in with her to be on call 24/7. This meant that his tiny one bedroomed flat was empty and it would be possible for me to kip down there for a short period until things were sorted out. That was fantastic, I would have a roof over my head and time to get to the bottom of all the problems.

It was a huge upheaval, of course, but in the meantime, I had to count my lucky stars that I wasn't living under a bridge somewhere. It was awful living in a dirty, noisy town and crying from morning till night not understanding really what was happening. My friend, in spite of his personal problems, was a huge moral support and started organising me as I was literally mentally incapacitated at that time and in the midst of a very heavy depression.

Through his contacts we were given the name of a lawyer and fixed an appointment to see her.

I had no other choice. I had been abandoned and Faby had no intentions of finding a solution but just wanted me to disappear forever.

CHAPTER 28

I had been given a couple of names of lawyers in Milan but because of where my house was, I was apparently under the jurisdiction of Monza and therefore had to get a lawyer that covered that area. So be it, we fixed an appointment with a lady lawyer in Monza, and Andy very kindly accompanied me as I was in no state to face the situation alone.

It was a small studio and very much in disorder but the people seemed very kind and very much on my side. This gave me some moral support and a bit of hope. I was told that what he was doing was illegal and that he should have left the house as I was unemployed and had nowhere to go. As it had been Faby who kicked me out, my lawyer suggested we try to sort things out in a consensual way as this would make the legal procedures a little quicker. I told her that even after all he and his family had done, I had always been willing to be civil to try and find a solution but this was not reciprocated. At that time, he hadn't even looked for his own lawyer. He couldn't be bothered to talk about a solution as he just wasn't interested. Hence, she suggested he come for an appointment and she could represent both of us. In the beginning, it seemed a good idea as I had no income, and he would pay her fee for both of us.

The lawyer that was supposed to be representing me actually worked in Milan and only helped out part-time in the studio in Monza and little by little, the Monza lawyer took over.

The lady who should have been my lawyer was very kind and understanding and gave me some hope of getting justice. She explained that the law required that the husband should keep his ex-wife at the same level of life as before and that an allowance was due and I should get my house back. However, with the takeover of the lady boss in

Monza, things didn't quite work out as they should have.

In the beginning, the boss seemed to know what she was doing and had some good ideas, but as each day went by, I saw that we were up a brick wall.

She kept pestering him to come in for a chat with no result so we had to get what information we could to be able to propose an agreement.

During the next weeks, she sent me all over the place to get documents and bank statements where possible in order to have a clear picture of his financial situation. Without this, no agreement could be proposed and he refused to cooperate.

My first task was the central bank in Milan, who are obliged to give out information to debtors enabling them to check their situation. As we had an idea that he had been giving most of his income to his family, as his wife, I was certainly involved. In fact, the Central Bank gave me a printout, which left me astounded.

There was a whole list of debts in my name of which I knew nothing.

Not only had my husband been keeping secrets from me, but the banks themselves had never informed me of anything, so much for women's rights. He had been getting letters from the various banks informing and threatening him, but no one had thought to notify me. I was just as responsible for his debts, unfortunately, as his wife but as his wife very little information was available!

I sent the Central Bank's printout to the lawyer, who went ballistic obviously. The information reported at least four bank accounts in his name only and that is the reason why I had never been informed about his loans. The fact that he had set up his own company with help from my father meant that he had been able to open all sorts of accounts in the company name without my knowledge and only now, because of his debts, were they being discovered.

This information gave us something to work on and my lawyer then sent me to the various banks mentioned to get an update and some explanations. That was easier said than done as although I was named on the debt, the bank accounts being in his name were private and it took a lot of running around for days to get the basic information with official requests from the lawyer without breaking any privacy laws.

Every day that went by there was new evidence and more shocks and each time she tried to speak with him he would deny everything and not be available for a face-to-face meeting.

It got to the point where she had to threaten him to come in and when he finally graced us with his presence and the documents were shoved in front of his face, he pretended that it was all untrue!

It was a nightmare. He had upped the mortgage on my house several times without telling me just to get cash for his little tart and her family and never repaid it. There were loans here and there and many private bank accounts in the company name where he had been paying out to his family and being able to hide it from me.

As if that wasn't enough, as I now had a different address, the banks suddenly started to inform me of the situation and I received copies of the menacing letters sent to my husband.

They told me to pay off his debts immediately. Well, why didn't they have the courtesy of informing me sooner? Now all of a sudden, it's my responsibility because they are having no luck contacting him? Incredible!

We had to fix several meetings, given the gravity of the situation that had come to light.

In one of the meetings my lawyer proposed that my moving to Andy's apartment should be made official and the town hall should be advised. This would make things easier for letters and various communications and she was also very worried about my state of health. She said that she would be a witness in court as to the fact that I had not been the one to leave the matrimonial home and, therefore would not influence the judge's decision. This seemed all above board and a good idea, as I certainly could not bear the thought of living under the same roof with this liar and continually undergoing his psychological abuse. He refused to leave my house and so the decision was accepted.

In this particular meeting, Andy came too, so there was a witness to her promise, which made me feel a little more at ease with the decision.

CHAPTER 29

I had already tried to explain to the sister in law what a liar Faby was but had only received a mouthful of insults and threats. I had also tried to make her see sense regarding the behaviour of her daughter, all to no avail.

Then, as if fate wanted to give me even more proof of her instability, the nasty little thing started stalking me and it went on for weeks.

The kid must be off her rocker to do such a thing.

She had been living like a princess with our income for years without my knowledge, hairdresser, beauty salon and designer clothes, all things which I couldn't afford! She had interfered for years, broken up my marriage, but that wasn't enough, she had to rub it in by stalking me. I was getting paranoid always looking over my shoulders to see if she was there. I had her cheshire cat grin in front of me all the time and it was a nightmare. The worst thing of all was her stalking me at the sports centre I used to go to.

I had been ill in the past and water therapy had been suggested to me as an alternative to medicine and it was a huge benefit. The kid used the gym in the same sports centre trying to make herself more attractive for her hobby of breaking up marriages. Her sole objective in life was ruining that of others and she would stop at nothing.

She would take great delight in spying on me and report my comings and goings to my ex. She would be up in the gym where there was a big window looking down on the pool and as soon as she saw me enter into the pool to do my exercises, she would run down at the speed of lightening to the changing rooms, come into the pool and get the lane as near to me as she could and make faces at me. As time went by I had to really control myself as I wanted to strangle her on the spot.

Any normal person who had ruined a marriage and stolen someone else's husband would have changed sports centres and have been embarrassed, but no not she. She would come right up to me and look me in the face and laugh. It took a lot of willpower to ignore her. This went on for weeks and on one occasion, I tried to stop her by talking to her. It was a useless attempt as she would have that annoying smirk on her face and tell me that she had done absolutely nothing wrong at all and that my husband was her rightful possession!

At that point, I had to have a word with the managers of the centre as the situation was getting out of hand. The family were just waiting for me to make a false move to get me into trouble. I had to resist. I asked the managers of the centre to keep her away from me, explaining briefly about the situation.

Once the news got out a few people would open up and tell me a few home truths about her. It's always too late, of course, having your suspicions confirmed afterwards but at least I now knew that I wasn't paranoid as my husband had tried to convince me in the past.

As far as he was concerned the kid could do no wrong. He was completely obsessed with her as she was with him, and still to this day, I have doubts as to whether she is his daughter, but even if that were the case the whole situation was weird. Her mother had three brothers and a brother-in-law but never did she behave with the other uncles as she did with my husband. It just wasn't normal for me and I couldn't accept it.

I was told by people at the centre that this wasn't the first time that she had acted in such a way. In fact, just a while ago, she had targeted another couple who came to the gym. She would pick on someone or something and it would become an obsession, just as my husband was her present sick obsession. She would stalk this poor guy and try to get him to leave his companion. In this particular case, he was more aware of being in the company of a raving lunatic and, after several weeks, managed to distance her in no uncertain terms. She would spy on him and as soon as he finished his session in the gym, she would follow him everywhere. On the way out, there is a stairway and a big mirror where you get to the reception to give in your locker key. She would keep her distance and then hide under the stairs to listen to what he was saying to the receptionist, then, acting out her insane jealousy, she would fly up the stairs accusing all and sundry who had dared to speak to him! She was so intent on spying on him that she never realised that from the reception they could see her in the big mirror hiding! She would become a demon and start bollocking the receptionist accusing her of all sorts of things and obviously got the name of a lunatic with the staff. When the poor guy finally managed to get rid of her, that is when she started out her insane campaign to get her hands on my husband. All the pieces of the puzzle are coming together now, although it is too late for me to do anything about it.

The managers at the sports centre were very understanding and, given her past and present behaviour, were more than willing to keep her away from me. Luckily for her I didn't have to make an official police report, which meant less stress for me.

CHAPTER 30

I started to get more and more threatening letters from the banks. They were all pretty nasty and said they were about to repossess my house if we didn't pay up.

According to the printout from the Central Bank he wasn't paying his part on our house and hadn't been for a long time. Incomes were disappearing without a trace and obviously going to his family.

I was very worried and needed to sell the house so I could get the debt paid, but he had refused.

I was so frustrated that without his permission, I couldn't even sell my own house, just what sort of laws are they here?

I sent a copy of the letters which kept coming to my lawyers. To my surprise, they just laughed. You don't have to worry about that, they said. It's normal procedure here in Italy, it will take them at least five years before they do anything about it!

It is such a strange country, I thought. He has swindled me legally, his family have taken everything away from me, the niece is a nut job and roams about trying to destroy lives, threatening legal letters that don't mean a thing, stalking and whatever. Why ever did I come to this country, for heaven's sake?

We started working on an agreement and each time we seemed to come to a reasonable solution, another lie or debt or problem emerged.

It was so nerve-racking. I mean why can't we just have the truth, get it over with and find a solution?

He was still trying to hide the truth even now which was more work for the lawyer and more time lost for me.

The information obtained also confirmed that there was yet another bank account open, which we didn't know about.

When I bought the house where he was now living he had asked a friend for a loan just to get started and had told me that it had been paid off in the first year of purchase. Well, surprise, surprise, we found out that to pay his friend back he had taken out yet another loan in a bank where the account was supposed to have been closed years ago. It was an account also in my name, which meant that the loan was also in my name and he had never told me.

After that, the lawyer asked about information regarding how much the house was worth as it would have to be sold and the gains split two ways. This was another sore point as not paying the mortgage for so long, the eventual sale of the house would just be enough to pay off the debt, so what exactly is he waiting for? The house, unfortunately was in joint names.

In Italy, there is what is called the "comunione dei beni." When a couple get married they can choose between the separate or joint ownership of assets and property.

When we got married I had my own flat in my name and when I bought our first slightly larger flat for us to start our life together he insisted that we use the "comunione dei beni." That should have been an alarm bell for me but of course, when you care for someone you don't think that they are going to swindle you, particularly when it is your own husband! If I had been a wealthy person, I could perhaps understand his greedy family but heavens all I had was my flat and had worked jolly hard to pay for that.

When my father gave him money to start up on his own I did seek advice from a lawyer friend who was very insistent that the house should go back in my name.

She explained that according to Italian law, if anything went wrong with his new business, we would still have a house to live in as any debts would be in his company name and the house being in my name was untouchable.

If he really cares for me and also having this possibility of starting up on his own then he is surely going to agree that this decision is common sense. No such luck, unfortunately. He had a fit and would not hear of taking his name off the property. Even when explaining that it was for our security, he would not budge. The problem was that without his consent, the law would not permit me to make a decision on my own, there was nothing I could do.

There have been so many similar situations where I should have been wary and just cannot understand now why I kept giving him so many chances to prove that he had his head on his shoulders. He was such a good actor and his lies seemed so feasible he just had me continually conned.

Having established that I was not allowed to sell my own house without his consent, we had to work on convincing him. He was asked to bring in all the documents regarding the purchase and mortgage on the house.

Having forced me out, all our various documents were with him in the house, and a lot of them had disappeared as I had already verified. However, he did very sulkily bring some of them in for us to study. It was no wonder that he was so reluctant to let us have any information, as these documents were beginning to paint a very cruel picture of exactly how incompetent and what a complete idiot he was. How could I have been fooled for all these years?

In any case, as the lawyer said, the house has to be sold. Not for gains, obviously but solely to be able to extinguish the debt.

She kept trying to draw up a draft of an agreement and asked him to go in alone so she could try and knock some sense into him.

I am not a lawyer, so I will have to trust the professionals, but I had a bad feeling about it.

Just as expected, he had brought out his bootlicking charm and she was completely taken in. He had shown her the pictures of the flat in Germany and all the work he had been doing and the next time I saw her, she went on and on about how wonderful he was and what a good job he had done. I couldn't believe that my own lawyer, a supposedly intelligent person, had been totally fooled. Of course, he had also given her his sob story about his mother and how he had to take care of her and therefore had nothing to give to me! So I got an earful about this wonderful person who didn't exist!

Lo and behold, the draft was ready almost immediately and of course, it was in his favour!

Up until this moment, everyone who knew about the situation told me to trust my lawyer, the situation was so bad that I didn't have any choice.

She was supposed to have contacted the banks on my behalf to get my name off the debts but had

made an agreement with only one bank where the account was in joint names and they promised both verbally and in writing that if I paid off one of the debts in this bank, my name would be cleared.

Having nothing more myself Andy allowed me to use the German account with the lawyer guaranteeing that Faby would pay it back short term. As Faby's Aunt had died in the meantime and left him her small house, he had this to sell and therefore, it was certain that he could pay Andy's loan. Another huge mistake as he later refused to sell his aunt's house as promised and never paid the debt, nor did the bank keep their word even though we had their promise in writing. I had a huge argument with the lawyer as it was her responsibility to follow up, but after the chat with Faby, she was beginning to wash her hands of everything that concerned me and now the debt was paid in his favour. Who cares. I was furious with her.

The banks are a law unto themselves; they hadn't kept their promise and my lawyer had done nothing.

At this point, I realised that my gut feeling was becoming a reality and contrary to all the advice from people outside the situation, I started looking for a new lawyer.

I found a big law firm in Milan, which had been recommended to me as a very competent establishment and showed them the agreement that my present lawyer was trying to make me sign.

They were absolutely horrified.

Apparently, the Monza lawyer had made a pig's ear of everything and had ruined my chances of getting any justice and I would now have to start all over again. According to the law, he had no right to force me out or take my keys away but the Monza lawyer giving me her word that it was all legit had ruined any possibility of me going back to my own house because too much time had gone by. They also confirmed that paying his debt to the bank was also a big mistake and she had worked solely in his favour. There were a whole list of complaints and astonishment at how a colleague of theirs could have been so stupid and I was strongly advised to revoke her authority with immediate effect before she did any more damage.

CHAPTER 31

It was all a bit overwhelming to find out how much damage she had done. If you can't trust your own lawyer, then just who can you trust. So many wasted months and I was at square one yet again with no job possibilities and no allowance. I should have left Andy's flat by a long time now as I was a guest on a short-term period so what to do?

I got an update about the real situation from my new lawyers and was disgusted to find out that the law gives no protection to people in dire straights. They explained that I had no rights to my own house any longer because of the huge mistake on the old lawyer's part. She had no right to oblige me to pay one of his debts from Andy's german account and should have followed up the agreement with the bank and got a proper agreement signed before giving up the money. Her proposal had covered all aspects of both Faby's wellbeing and all of his family and had made him out to be a hero looking after his poor old mother and maintaining his little tart. I had basically worked all my life for their benefit without knowing it. Studying the Central Bank printout more in-depth, they informed me that I had been put on the blacklist in all the banks in the whole of Italy. This was again because of that damned "comunione dei beni." The fact that we were joint owners made me responsible for all his debts even though I had never been informed and my husband had done all his dastardly work behind my back. I'm on a blacklist; there's a first time for everything!

The new lady's lawyer said she was willing to take on my case, and at that point, I had to agree. So much time had been lost, and now we would have to begin again.

The new law firm wasn't perfect either, as they also sent me on a wild goose chase for weeks on end, trying to get information from the various banks. I was treated like dirt in the banks, and even when I explained that I knew nothing of what he had been doing and was trying to find a solution for everyone, they were still nasty. I had many arguments with a lot of the bank managers as I had to start standing up for myself. That was tough and I got nowhere.

The old lawyer was also behaving badly and was obviously offended that she had been sacked.

My new lawyers needed all the documents she had been working on so they could start off again and hopefully put things right, and we had a hard time getting them back.

After many arguments and threats, we eventually got everything that she had been working on so that the new law firm could get up to speed.

Andy himself was one of the many people that questioned my decision to change lawyers as given the situation, it seemed that there was very little I could do. Italian law gives the impression of being on the side of the criminal as many of Faby's actions had been on the verge of legal/non-legal but after hearing the opinion of the new law firm Andy was just as shocked as I and said thank goodness that I had had a sixth sense about the situation and changed lawyer just in time.

I begged them to move quickly as so much time had already gone by and the more time that passed the more time Faby had to get rid of my few assets. He had already put so much in the name of his family without my permission, which meant that, according to Italian law, it was no longer mine. How can this be that he just does what he wants and gets away with it? So much for a wife having rights! It seemed that as his wife, I had no say in anything and he could do exactly what he wanted and the law protected him as well. I was beginning to see that over the years, both he and his family had been swindling me and taking everything I owned and it was a well-thought-out project. Little by little everything was being transferred to them so that I couldn't get my hands on anything that was once mine. It was a diabolical plan.

I would have to trust my lawyers yet again, but this time, I tried to be more forceful and kept insisting they get a move on. They, on the contrary, preferred to keep trying for a consensual solution, which was never going to work. They also kept trying to fix meetings for an informal chat, but the months went by and he was never available. Although I reputed them as a very good law firm and they certainly knew the law and were capable of doing their job, however, they did not know just what sort of devil he and his family were and I had to insist constantly that they listen to me. Another nightmare is trying to speak to overworked lawyers with little time and other more important clients. Only when I went right over the top shouting and threatening to sack them too did I manage to get my call returned. That's just so typical over here, everything is literally a fight to get your rights even just a simple thing like a phone call being returned.

Anyhow, after months of investigations, the situation was drastic. It seemed that he had forged my signature on many documents to make me guarantor of his debts. I know during my depression period when he was psychologically abusing me that he would bring home papers and make me sign them so it's more than probable that some of them, unfortunately I had signed under duress. On the other hand there were many other documents of which I knew absolutely nothing and had definitely been forged.

My lawyer told me that it would be difficult to prove the forgery and so yet again he would probably get away scot free and there was nothing we could do about it.

It was one thing after another, the debts, the mortgage, forged signature, banks not respecting agreements, being on the blacklist, it seemed to be never-ending, never a tiny piece of positive news.

He was doing everything he could to spite me and couldn't see that he was also spiting himself.

My lawyers informed me that the credit cards had been written off and it would be years before I could have one again because of the blacklist situation. It would also be dangerous to open up a bank account in my name as I was still legally his wife and that meant that any earnings I might make in the future could be taken away from me to pay his debts.

Can it get any worse?

Any normal person would seek professional help and get a plan of action as to how the debts could be paid but no not he.

He was so angry seeing me finally standing up to him and fighting that he punished me with a hate campaign which was horrible.

He literally went round to every single person I knew and slandered me.

All my so-called friends in Germany started turning their backs on me and little by little no one would speak to me or keep in touch. This was needless to say not only disappointing but also very hurtful. People who in the beginning had shown great friendship and loyalty towards me were now disappearing. I even received some very nasty messages from some of my once so-called friends accusing me of all sorts defending him.

Another discovery was a huge amount of money that was going out from our household to pay the flat where his mother was living.

He had bought the place a few years ago, which had been yet another decision made with his nasty sister-in-law behind my back. Some of his friends who were just on speaking terms assured me that he had promised the flat to little madam and as soon as the wicked witch died, the flat would be hers. When I found out about the purchase years back I begged him to at least put the flat in his or my name. The reason for my insistence was that according to the law, when the old witch died, it would be automatically left to next of kin. And who are the next of kin? Cry baby brother of course and himself. This would mean that his brother yet again would receive a windfall without ever having lifted a finger and little madam would have her nice little city flat and be independent. Although he was paying with our money the house legally belonged to the old witch and that was a crafty move. There was nothing I could do, it was too late.

All sorts of news started to filter my way. I had had many suspicions over the years but no proof and every time I faced Faby and asked for explanations he had become such a good actor that I believed him.

The messages kept arriving from people in Germany who would take great delight in giving me tidbits of news now and again. Every couple of months he was giving himself a nice long weekend and a luxury holiday instead of paying off his debts. I couldn't believe it. Hotel, restaurants, etc and really living it up. He was corrupting the whole circle of friends that I had. He would take presents and go round making up all sorts of stories about me and as I couldn't possibly afford a holiday, I wasn't present to defend myself. At one point I received a message telling me to call the bank in Germany. I started getting worried and called to ask what was happening. Apparently, he had been for yet another holiday and had tried to loot Andy's account. I was flabbergasted. He was on holiday spending stolen money or money that had been acquired under false pretences and was desperate. Thankfully, the account was in my name. It was the only positive thing that the old lawyer had insisted on and that was that Faby take his name off that particular account as the money wasn't ours. The rules are much harsher in Germany, and the bank thankfully had respected the fact that his name was not on the account and they sent him away with his tail between his legs. He was willing to steal yet again with no scruples whatsoever. It was alarming to think that I just didn't know the person with whom I had been living for all these years.

CHAPTER 32

By now, we had accumulated documents going back at least ten years and it was evident that I had been used from day one. I had been job hunting since he kicked me out, but for a woman of my age, it was almost impossible. No one was interested and all the jobs were for youngsters.

Because of the situation, even if I was lucky enough to find a job, I would have to work for cash; otherwise, my money would be taken away from me. In a nutshell, if I didn't work, I couldn't live, and if I did work, I still couldn't live as all my earnings would go to pay the debts he had accumulated on behalf of his family and they would benefit from my earnings. It was a vicious circle and a never-ending story. Doors were being closed in my face everywhere I turned and his family were continually benefitting.

We had tried to get my name off the debts in every legal way possible to no avail and so no chance of making a clean start. Faby did everything he could to put obstacles in the way and keep his secrets not just from me but from his family too to maintain appearances. There was nothing else I could do but to insist on going to court and let a judge decide.

I would have to live the rest of my life hiding any future earnings under my mattress!

The hope of an agreement before going to court was off the table, which meant the first hearing was just for the legal separation. Regarding the economic side and trying to get back what was officially mine would be a different court case and that would be a long battle. I was told it could take anything from five to ten years and of course by that time he would have transferred everything to his family so there was never going to be any justice.

What a depressing situation and just what sort of law is it over here that supports the wrongdoings of the likes of him?

In any case, I just wanted to be free of him and even more so of his evil family and so I insisted that the lawyers go ahead with the request for a hearing.

We went ahead with the request and had a five-month wait. Given the slowness of the legal system that was actually quite good but still far too long given the year and a half already wasted. In this particular hearing the judge would only be able to give his approval regarding the separation and, eventually, an allowance.

My lawyers explained that the judge would probably give his approval for the separation, which would mean that from that date onwards, any other debts would not be my responsibility, so for that alone, it was worth doing.

However, as for hoping for an allowance or getting my house back the judge would only consider the facts. My ex could prove that he had nothing at the end of the month and therefore I should expect nothing!

So much for a joint marriage, and so much for being married to an Italian and, worse still in Italy. Evidently no women's rights and no protection for people below the poverty level. I was being treated as a second-class citizen.

In a nutshell, my future was sink or swim, the situation was catastrophic.

After the psychological abuse and being belittled for years it was my word against his. There was no proof, no-one would come forward and nobody would believe me.

I had been forced out of my own home and had no right to go back because of the incompetence of the first lawyer. If I tried he could call the police and get me arrested! I couldn't even go back into my own house and collect my personal belongings if he wasn't "kind" enough to give me an appointment! Even if I won the lottery, I couldn't open a bank account in my name as what is mine is his and the banks could also claim everything to pay off his debts. He had gradually been transferring my assets and putting them in his family's name. I was not entitled to an allowance, not even a pittance just to eat but he could spend all his wage on his family or nice holidays proving that at the end of the month he had nothing.

Where exactly are my rights in this country and do I have any at all? Up until now, at least in my case what is mine is his and what is his is his! Does that seem right?

At the end of the day, he has legally swindled me of everything I have ever worked for and more. I ask myself what the point is of having a lawyer if they can do nothing?

A new law had recently been approved which gives lawyers the right to investigate the tax situation and any possible fraud. Previously, one would have to engage a private investigator which costs thousands of euros whereas now the lawyers following a case can look into everything themselves. This procedure could not begin however until the day after the court hearing which was frustrating but at least a tiny piece of good news.

We would get him investigated for tax evasion, the people from whom he had obtained money under false pretences would sue him and we would also be opening a case against his family for moral damages.

All comforting words but it remains to be seen if my lawyers actually keep their word and if any results come out of it.

All things considered, I have been very lucky to have been a guest and looked after by my friend and his family. I ask myself what happens to other battered or abused wives who find themselves on the streets in this country, having looked for shelter myself to no avail.

As the Italians say, the family is sacred - "la famiglia è sacra." It certainly is, except for the fact that a foreign wife is not considered family!

After two years of time wasting and a complete farce we finally had the court hearing for the legal separation.

The separation actually went through and the judge ordered him to pay me monthly sums until I was able to find a job and get myself back on my feet.

Surprise, surprise, he paid the first month and disappeared.

After which, the next years were reporting him, more court cases and a slowness that was unbelievable.

In the meantime, of course there was also the divorce to sort out.

That also did eventually go through and with that the monthly sum was reduced.

By this time, I had changed lawyer yet again because of the total frustration of having to deal with such incompetence and couldn't care less attitude. So much time wasted. If I hadn't have had a roof over my head and was desperately in need it all would have been too late. The justice system protects the criminals and that was so obvious.

The hearing for the divorce was to say the least, painful. My new lawyer never showed up once and always sent a practising lawyer who was no help whatsoever.

As usual my ex had a way with people which was believable. The judge was a woman and fell totally for his charm. The intern that my wonderful lawyer had sent had specifically told me to keep quiet during the hearing and that she would speak for me. The judge started almost insulting me, saying that my poor husband was looking after his elderly mother, stories that he was very good at telling, and that I should be ashamed of myself and get a job. I looked at the intern who ignored me and continued to keep quiet. What should I do? Reply and defend myself or hope that she would do her job. At the end I knew there was no point as I could see that the lady judge was completely taken with Faby, it was useless. The monthly sum was halved and I was told to get off my backside and stop taking advantage of this poor boy! However, I got my divorce - at least that.

CHAPTER 33

During this time the mutual friend Andy, who eventually told me that he too had been swindled and for this reason had taken my side, invited me to move into a spare room he had in a small mountain village where he was going to live.

Given my situation, no full-time job, no maintenance sums coming in and a huge rescue dog that I had taken under my wing, I accepted the offer.

Years went by of legal hassle trying to get my monthly sums without results. This became no longer a civil hearing, as they say but a case for criminal court. He had now officially become a criminal.

He had put what he had stolen under different names and managed to hide everything, working for cash so no trace. According to the law over here, he had nothing and couldn't pay poor thing and that was it. Yet again, protection for the criminal and the victim could just get on with it.

Unbelievable!

His lawyer was a right bitch, they really did make a wonderful couple. Him, a liar and a cheat. Her, a liar and a cheat. A match made in heaven I would say.

I was so naive in the way I was brought up to believe that in court, one had to tell the truth. No way, completely the opposite. The more you could fool the judge the better.

This lady lawyer, well calling her a lady is actually not the right term but I could get very vulgar, in any case she lied through her teeth making up any excuse she could which had nothing to do with the case but trying to get the judge's sympathy. It was pathetic and I asked myself that if I could see it why couldn't a judge that should have, in theory, a load of experience.

No can do yet again. This situation went on for years with court case after court case and this little bitch making up all sorts of stories to get cases postponed on the smallest piece of bullshit possible.

Not just her that messed things up but the whole legal system. Again totally unbelievable. Until you get involved in the legal system in Italy nobody would believe you. The times I went for a hearing and there was no judge. Today there is a strike or today the judge is ill or today we don't have another judge available or the latest, the judge is expecting a baby and can't come today - really????

So I would lose days getting to the courthouse for absolutely nothing but having to pay my lawyer for his time and each time, it wasn't a question of waiting a week to get the next hearing but at least six months each time. No wonder things don't work over here and are so long-winded.

The only good thing I can say about the whole thing becoming a criminal offence is that I had to get a criminal lawyer and this time he was really good. A bit late but finally someone who knew his job. How many lawyers had I been through and had to pay before finding someone that actually not only did his job but knew about the law too. Seems incredible but 99 percent of lawyers don't even know the law, they just lie and make things up completely out of context wasting so much time.

To cut a very long story short the years went by with his lawyer making up so many things to get the cases put off hoping that everything would fall into statute of limitations that I could have lived two lives and now after more than ten years the final sentence where he will be sentenced to six months probation without having paid a penny and after all the court cases won but without an actual result.

CHAPTER 34

Another huge disappointment was Andy. Another initially very kind and charming Italian who I had always considered my best friend. In fact, as mentioned before, when my wonderful husband threw me out and threatened to kill me, I would have been homeless if it hadn't been for him.

As he had also been swindled too he obviously took my side and offered me a room.

At first, we lived in a city near to Milan and then we moved to a small mountain area.

This was his dream and not mine, but humility is a must when someone gives a helping hand.

The town was very cut off having no public transport so at the beginning, he would have to give me a lift for appointments out of town which he seemed to do quite willingly.

The mountain people are hard working, honest people but very closed and do not let outsiders in, so impossible to make friends.

The only work available was for family and friends who were born there so to earn my keep I became his domestic, cook, cleaner etc.

Apart from his kindness, he was probably the most lazy man I have ever met. He had never worked in his life saying that he suffered from anxiety and his father had always protected him, buying him a house and paying the bills so his spoilt little brat didn't have to suffer!

In the beginning, I tried to put up with it as, after all he was giving me a roof over my head and I had to pay back in some way.

After a while however, it started to become very annoying seeing someone sitting on a chair from morning till night and watching me work my butt off.

He is another typical example of an Italian "man" that is not a man at all.

I would spend a lot of time in the kitchen preparing all sorts of lovely meals and trying to spoil him and show my gratitude. He was always tired as doing nothing all day is very tiring!

His mother had spoilt him rotten, so of course, he didn't know how to cook or hardly even change a light bulb, permit me to say.

Most evenings, he would ask me when dinner was ready, and I would tell him that he just had to wait another ten minutes and all would be ready. His reply was that he was hungry now and couldn't possibly wait. He would open up an enormous packet of crisps and down the lot.

When dinner was ready he would look at the food and say that it looked very nice, but he was not hungry anymore. After hours in the kitchen preparing, this eventually got on my nerves and I told him that if he wasn't hungry he should tell me and avoid me spending hours cooking and wasting so much. That didn't go down very well and kept repeating that it was his house and therefore could do as he pleased.

This went on for a long time and each month he got worse and worse, taking me for granted and sometimes being very insulting. I couldn't believe this was a complete replica of what had happened to me previously. I really had thought that he was a charming person, but of course, until you live under the same roof you never really know.

When I accepted to go up and live in the mountains with him it was most of all for my beloved dog Snowy so he could have a garden and a good life. A beautiful Maremma sheepdog. I had saved him from the same situation that I had been through and wasn't a puppy anymore. He had been beaten and abandoned and was extremely aggressive. Anyone that has dogs will understand that his behaviour was out of pure fright and distrust of human beings quite rightly so.

He fell in love with me immediately and I did with him and was my rock from day one getting me through depression and understanding me as I tried to do for him. I have had more affection and love from Snowy during the years than from any man in my life. They say owners and their dogs are the same and in symbiosis and in this case it really was true . Dogs know who love them immediately and I was the only one he didn't try to bite out of fear. He was difficult to handle in the beginning and eventually I went to different trainers for help. The first trainers told me to send him back to the kennel where he came from and let him die there as there was absolutely no hope. One trainer wanted to give him sedatives making it easier for him to train can you believe it and another who came to meet him was nearly eaten alive as Snowy hated him immediately. One of the trainers worked with the boss who only went onto television shows here in Italy and didn't train anymore and was very successful. This success was due to the fact that he either trained puppies which anyone can do or sheepdogs who find training fun and are very receptive. When his colleague gave his report about almost being eaten alive his boss replied he only trained one hundred percent certainties so he could go on television and say how wonderful he was.

I finally found an expert in aggressive dogs and started with him. Snowy attacked him immediately going for his private parts! At this point the guy immediately saw what there was to do. For the first time a genuine expert willing to help and not one of these know it alls that doesn't actually know anything. He put his protective suit on - the ones the police use when they are doing dog training and we started. He was very honest and actually trained me to be able to understand Snowy better and how to handle him. He then said that he had done all he could and that I should now continue with what I had learnt. He would never be perfect because of what he had gone through but now I was able to go ahead with more confidence. One of the very few honest people I have ever met in this country.

Going back to Andy, it was never ending complaints about my dog of course because he had nothing else to do but find fault with everything. It got extremely depressing hearing complaints and insults every single day and sometimes I would not have made it if it hadn't have been for the enormous bond that my dog and I had and got me out of the house away from the creep.

Many people, who luckily have not experienced psychological abuse don't understand what we go through unfortunately and just tell you to pick yourself up and get on with it. The police will not intervene and it is the same old story - "Madam, until he kills you we can not do anything" as it is your word against his and you are totally abandoned to get on with it whatever the outcome.

The situation became unbearable and many of you who are asking why I didn't get out is simply for my devotion to Snowy. He was happy there. The rents in this country are very high and unfortunately they are so far behind that it is almost impossible to to find a flat that accepts dogs unless it is your own house of course. Even when you see a rent with "animali ammessi" which means "pets allowed" you call and they say it's fine if you have a Chihuahua but good heavens no, not a Maremma sheepdog weighing 53 kilos - just think of the damage it could do! Well actually small dogs very often do more damage than the big giant dogs like mine so you evidently don't understand dogs.

Anyway it was an impossibile situation and I tried to resist for his happiness.

As always things made a turn for the worse and history started to repeat itself from my time in Milan. After many years of being friends very successfully he suddenly started to turn even more violent with his words and as had already happened before the threats started coming. He kept giving me ultimatums saying that if I didn't sleep with him it would be the worse for me and he would kick me out and leave me to die in the streets.

We had been friends for years before we came up to the mountains so what is going on after all this time?

I had always seen him as a friend and in no way given him any particular behaviour to make him think otherwise. To get to the point he became very violent verbally and put me in situations that were impossibile to handle.

He even started to accuse me of loving my dog more than him and scenes of jealousy would happen that should have been saved for the theatre. Well of course I love my dog more than him. He was just a friend. My dog was my life and my saviour and had been for years now.

Obviously I started to look for somewhere but it was the same old story. With a big dog on my hands nobody would give me the time of day.

I knew things were at the limit and we would be kicked out but I still couldn't find a lodgings anywhere. Living with him as a friend or working guest should we say I had no rights yet again and in fact the day came when he brutally kicked me out and there was nothing I could do.

Spoilt brat not getting his way and yet again out on the streets.

My dog by this time was getting elderly and having difficulty walking but he didn't hesitate to throw him out like a sack of rubbish. So much cruelty from these men that it really is unbelievable at times. A poor innocent creature being treated like this. Thankfully I managed to get him and we went to a girlfriends who put us up for a while and Snowy managed to recuperate his strength.

I have had many telling offs from people saying it is all my fault and a dog is just a dog - just put him down and don't sacrifice your own life. It is not something I can do and would rather live on the streets rather than abandon him, that is out of the question.

As i have already mentioned, mountain villages are tight knit and as I was not born here nearly everyone washed their hands of me and my situation and found myself abandoned yet again by society. I can count on one hand the really exceptional people here that really tried to help me not be homeless again and although without results will be forever grateful for them trying in any case.

So this is Italy. A wonderful place to visit with beautiful countryside, mountain and sea areas. Wonderful food, wine and cheeses and lots of hospitality. However, living is quite a different matter. Never get married if there is a mother-in-law, never get involved with the justice system, and don't hope that the police force will be of any help in any circumstances.

As for the rest of it.

Happy holidays!

www.ingramcontent.com/pod-product-compliance
Lightning Source LLC
Chambersburg PA
CBHW061220070526
44584CB00029B/3911